the Power of Touch

the Power
of Touch

Phyllis K. Davis

Hay House, Inc.
Carson, CA

THE POWER OF TOUCH
by Phyllis K. Davis

Copyright © 1991 by Phyllis K. Davis

Library of Congress Catalog Card No. 90-80705
ISBN: 0-937611-91-3

Library of Congress Cataloging-in-Publication Data

Davis, Phyllis K., 1938–
     The power of touch / Phyllis K. Davis.
         p.   cm.
     ISBN 0-937611-91-3 (pbk.)
     1. Touch—Psychological aspects.   2. Touch—Therapeutic use.
I. Title.
BF275.D38   1991
152.1'82—dc20   90-80705
                                                                                    CIP

Internal design by John K. Vannucci
Typesetting by Freedmen's Typesetting Organization,
Los Angeles, CA 90004

92 93 94 95 96   10 9 8 7 6 5 4 3 2
First Printing, March 1991
Second Printing, August 1992
Published and Distributed in the United States by

Hay House, Inc.
1154 E. Dominguez St.
P. O. Box 6204
Carson, CA 90749-6204 USA

Printed in the United States of America on Recycled Paper

recycled paper

Contents

Preface and Acknowledgements

 Just as expression of love is inhibited in our society, so is our touching behavior. Touch is not only a biological need but a communication tool. Touch is a language that can communicate more love in five seconds than five minutes of carefully chosen words.

It took me 14 years to finish my undergraduate degree and yet, when I began teaching English and coaching forensics and debate, I was still pretty idealistic. That didn't last long. How could I teach when the students weren't in a frame of mind to learn? To most of them, anything and everything were more important than school subjects. Many were often too emotionally upset to even make a pretense of paying attention. One day, after trying to calm several students enough to stop crying and just sit in the classroom, I knew something needed to be done and I had an idea. I made an appointment with the principal, Dr. Larry Clark to discuss the problem.

I went armed with outlines, rationales, objectives and a plan to return to school in order to qualify myself to teach a class about how to cope with emotions, people and life events. That wonderful man listened to what I wanted to do and said, "Yes, you can do it." I was stunned. "But . . . but," I explained, "you haven't even seen my rationale or anything." "I have faith in you," he simply replied.

So InterPersonal Communication (I.P.C.) was born. That summer I pored over the few materials then available and took a brief seminar at Central Missouri State University from Dr. Malloy Gould. In July as my father lay in his hospital bed, dying with cancer, I sat with him nights, worked on the I.P.C. course outline, and thought about our times together. I remembered his embraces, remembered how when I was five and had hurt my side badly, he had carried me close to him on a pillow. I thought a great deal about love and how closely touch was aligned with it.

For the next six years, 15 to 20 seniors per I.P.C. class gathered daily with me at the appointed times. We came together and talked and learned and touched one another deeply. These were challenging, frightening and beautiful experiences and I am grateful to each and every student for sharing themselves with me. It was truly a magnificent gift. We learned about love and sex, about death and communication. We talked about our feelings and learned how to accept them. We discovered that we really weren't so different from one another after all. We learned about *touching*. When I occasionally meet one of those former I.P.C. students now, our arms automatically open to hug each other. I miss those classes and those special people.

In the classroom we touched a lot; outside we were more careful because as one student put it, "People outside here don't really understand all this." I *wanted* those "people outside" to understand.

In a survey asking our school's graduates then in college or beyond what the most valuable preparatory courses were, there were more write-in votes for I.P.C. (it wasn't listed as a course selection) than any other subject. It seemed something important was happening in the I.P.C. classroom that was preparing the students for life.

The research for this book began during this period as part of a challenge in a graduate research and statistics course. I was told that touching was a "soft" subject (no pun was intended) and that I would be unable to find hard data to support my thesis that touching was a valuable adjunct to teaching and would help students to learn. I *was* able to show that however, and later did my Master's Thesis on nonverbal communication (including touching) in the classroom. I applied what I learned from my research in both my personal life and in the classroom with amazing results.

Over the years, I've received numerous calls and letters from students testifying to the power of touch in their lives. I continued to work with the area of touch in workshops with adults, married couples, singles and high school students.

I left teaching two years after finishing an interdisciplinary degree in psychology, counseling and interpersonal communication. Dr. Clark, who had been so supportive had moved on, the back-to-the-basics movement was in full swing and quite frankly, I was tired. Tired of fighting year after year the same battle to keep the class size small enough to accomplish our goals, and at times justify keeping the class at all. I was caught in a maelstrom of forces beyond my control. I turned my beloved I.P.C. over to my friend and colleague, Debbie Premoe and moved on.

Since time was often brief as I worked with private counseling clients and conducted seminars, I often longed for an easily readable, yet fully explanatory book on touching that I could recommend to my clients and participants whether they were in relationships, married, parents or parents-to-be, or simply the touch avoidant— for all those who didn't understand their fear of touch, their need for touch and the societal taboos against touch as well as for those who were simply interested in self-growth. I searched the bookshelves for such a book and finally decided I'd have to write it myself.

For seven years the primary research and notes for this book languished in the top left hand drawer of my file cabinet beside my desk. I had labeled it "Hopes and Dreams." I tried valiantly to write but there were so many interruptions and, seemingly, more urgent demands upon my time.

Then there came a time in my life when I began to feel an urgent need to "finish" things, and so I wrote long overdue letters, cleaned out closets, completed projects, called people, fulfilled some long term promises and still the file cabinet seemed to sit and stare at me as if to say, "Well, is it time yet?"

Finally, one June day as my son, Philip, was driving me to Des Moines, Iowa to do a management workshop for hospital supervisors, I was relaxing, skimming some books on the right brain when suddenly I was seized with the idea to go to some isolated place and either write the book or not write it. Whatever happened, it would be finished.

I called a friend, Natalie Zook, and asked about renting her cabin that we had previously used for week long retreats for women. She graciously agreed. So I set aside a precious ten days and set out, in August, for western Colorado. I drove for two days and arrived at the cabin, located in a rather secluded valley, altitude 7,000 feet, high above Quartz Creek, and set into the side of a mountain. I unloaded boxes of books, papers, typewriter, cassette player, containers of music tapes, food for a week and so on in a frenzy of activity, stopping only to gulp the wonderfully refreshing and pure mountain water between the twelve trips up and down 22 steps.

I set up my workplace in front of the 20 foot windows that composed two sides of the cabin and eagerly laid out all my materials. What I couldn't find were the forty typed pages and outline I had painstakingly already completed. I called home, certain those pages had just been left in the bottom of the file drawer. My dear husband, J.C. looked, and looked. He later told me he had gone through eight file drawers, one piece of paper at a time. To this day, I still don't know what happened to those typed pages.

With only one week remaining, I had to start over. I was dismayed. I walked; I read (eight books during the week); I sat beside Quartz Creek; I looked out the windows; I slept; I sunbathed till I was too burned to go out anymore; and one day Scarlet Riegel came to the cabin and gave me a massage. And in between all these activities, I wrote.

I finished the manuscript in the early hours of the morning I was to leave—or rather, it seemed the manuscript finished itself as I just tried to keep up with the movement of the typewriter keys.

On my way home I stopped off in Colorado Springs

to see Barbara Harlow, a longtime friend. She had a new playtoy, *The Book of Runes*, which describes runes as a reintroduction of an ancient oracle. I drew just one. It was called "Harvest" and then I knew the ground had been prepared, the seeds were all planted and I only needed to wait in patience for the reaping.

This book is the fruit of my labor and the harvest of one period of my life.

I wish to express my gratitude and love for all the people I have named for your help, support or encouragement. You have all truly touched my heart and my life.

In addition, I wish to recognize Dr. Jerry Winsor, who, along with Malloy Gould, was a mentor during my years at the university. It was Jerry who encouraged my nonacademic writing while Malloy acted as though I was thoroughly capable.

My family was patient with my activities and encouraging, so thank you, sons Jaye and Philip, and husband, J.C.

My sister, Patty (Trish) McFarland read the first draft of the manuscript and gave me helpful ideas and continues her nurturing support.

Cathy Thogmorton did her usual competent job of the first copyediting and my best friend, Nita Nolan used her magic flying hands to put the manuscript on computer disc and has been available to discuss, cuss and sometimes just listen.

Cindy Norman created the drawing for the largest tactile areas represented in the brain.

Another person to whom I am eternally grateful is John Steven Finney—wherever he is now—a writer himself, from whom I learned and learned and learned.

My parents, had they lived, would have been so proud to read this book and know I learned from them also.

Love and Light to all the wonderful friends and other people who have come to me at various times and interacted, guided, healed or loved me.

To all my former I.P.C. students, thank you.

Blessings!

Phyllis Koehler Davis
July 14, 1990
Lee's Summit, Missouri

Introduction ○ How Do You Feel About "Touch"?

These questions about touch are for you to answer (either silently or on another sheet of paper) before you read the book, based on your present opinions and experience. They were developed because I discovered in my classes that most people had never really thought much about touch. By answering as truthfully as possible before you read, the book could quite probably be of more personal value.

There is another copy of this questionnaire in the appendix if you wish to answer the questions again upon completion of the book or if you feel that someone else could benefit from it.

1. What *first* comes to mind when you think of the word "touching?"

2. How would you define "touching?"

3. Whom do you touch regularly (outside of sexual activity)?

4. On what part of the body do you usually touch people? List the people and the body parts.

5. Who touches you regularly?

6. Where are you usually touched? List the people and the areas they touch.

7. When do you usually want or like to be touched?

8. How do you usually want or like to be touched?

9. Are you ever aware of a physical need to be touched outside of sexual need?

10. When do you think others want or need to be touched?

11. Think about your parents and explain their touch behavior with you;
with each other;
with others.

12. What restrictions or inhibitions do you feel about touching others? For example, what about time, place, occasion, person, daylight or dark?

13. Do you remember any particular time or times when touch especially helped you. Briefly explain and how it helped.

14. Why do you think people don't touch more?

15. Why don't *you* touch more?

16. How would you describe (use adjectives) the kind of nonsexual touch you might want?

17. Has your need for touch increased or decreased with age? Why do you think this has happened?

18. At what age was the need for touch greatest for you? Why do you think this was?

19. Do you believe males or females touch others more often? Are touched the most?

20. At what age do you think touching ought to be stopped or limited? Explain.

21. What do you think of the health prescription: "three hugs a day"? How many hugs do you get a day? How many do you want?

22. If you have sex with a regular partner which would you prefer, the act of sex or just holding and stroking and cuddling? Why would you prefer this?

23. If you could tell your partner honestly, with no holds barred, two things about touching and lovemaking that you want him or her to know for your benefit, what would they be?

1 ○ The Loving Touch

From the heart comes love and from love comes touching. Please touch me.

 Love is mysterious, wondrous, bewitching, healing, enchanting, magic. It is powerful! Touch is powerful, too. Love can be affectionate, kind, tender, compassionate or passionate. So can touch. My message for you can be summed up in three words: *touching is loving.* Observe closely and you will see that not much touching occurs in our society. The problem is that it requires close observation to reveal that touching is relegated to limited gestures, to a limited number of people, to a limited extent. You may also observe, as I have, that much touching behavior borders on the surreptitious. Why are we so limited in our touching?

The answer is social consciousness. Our society inhibits expressions of love and, as a result, touching behavior. How sad for us. How sad for the millions of human beings who would give anything to have what one person's beloved cat or dog gets in the loving and touching department—even for one day. How ironic that animals in our society receive what we, as human beings, need so much. Of course, animals, too, need touching.

1

But, in turn, they give lots of touching to their young and to each other. Many animals lick and stroke their offspring when they are hurt. But, many parents simply say to their children, "Don't cry," and then stick on a band-aid.

As I look back at the first two-thirds of my life, I see what, in my ignorance, I did in the name of loving and, more importantly, what I did not do that could have been loving. I realize that although I am not always perfect in my loving expression, I can do much to enrich my life and the life of others. I have always believed that how I love myself becomes how I love others. The search for love begins as a journey within and manifests later in our outer demonstrations. Both the inner journey and the outer expressions can be worked on simultaneously. We can cope with our own hang-ups, our own pain, our own emotions and at the same time help those who come into our lives with their hang-ups, their pain, their emotions—*and* their touching needs.

It is quite possible, as you may already know, to accept and believe something on an intellectual level and yet reject it on an emotional level. If this is the case, the intellectual knowledge, the acceptance, the belief, will not manifest in your life. However, I do not ask for your belief, but your thoughts. If the information and ideas presented about touching appeal to you, then for a space of time, hold them in your mind and heart without believing—or disbelieving. Allow them to draw to you an inner certainty or to disappear. There is much about the need and the power of touch that cannot be scientifically proven. So you are free to accept or reject these concepts. For myself, I have studied and ruminated about and explored the subject of touch, I have then done as I just suggested you do and I have that inner certainty.

As you read about personal experiences, research, arguments, and anecdotes, observe any points at which you encounter emotional resistance or skepticism. Make mental or written notes concerning your feelings and patterns of behavior as you read about the need for touch or the expressions of loving through touch. This process will tell you much about yourself. This book is not meant to be read on an intellectual level; it is meant to touch you inside. It is meant to touch your heart.

As a counselor and communications instructor, I teach my clients and students that the basis of emotional well-being, of self-esteem, is love—love of the self and love for others. In one of my group counseling sessions, I asked the participants to relax and then to visualize the small person that exists inside each of them who needs to be loved.

One participant, Marge, later talked about her experience. She said that when her children were babies, she spent her time thinking, reading, and watching TV and considered her children's demands irritating. She never enjoyed just holding, rocking, or being close them. Yet, in her visualization of loving herself, she experienced the joy of being tenderly held and rocked, warmly cuddled, and enjoying the closeness and the skin-to-skin contact of touching. She cried as she realized that she had deprived her children of such a basic need, of something she so obviously needed for herself. (We'll speak later on about this type of guilt.)

Touch plays an important, if ambivalent, role in our lives. In groups, touch exercises elicit widespread positive responses that illustrate our deep yearning for physical contact. They also cause fear. In workshops for singles on touching, I lead groups through a number of touching experiences, ranging from ordinary, everyday types of touching behavior to more tender and intimate nonsexual touching. Since I usually work with large groups and try to see to it that everyone participates in the exercises with a a partner (I just assume people come to learn and how better to learn than by direct experience), I ask those without partners to raise their hands so that they can find someone to pair off with. Invariably, it will be the men who will either not raise their hands or who seem unable to make the effort to pair off until I help them do so.

During one workshop, I had made the rounds of the room a number of times, pairing off people, when I noticed way in the back, leaning against a wall, a man. He was good looking, young and obviously trying to be inconspicuous. Since everyone else was paired off, I asked two young women if they would include him in their group. They agreed.

This particular exercise involved placing both hands lightly and gently along the jaw and chin of one's partner and then smiling softly into the other's eyes. I call this face-cupping the "tenderness touch." At the end of the exercise, while the partners discussed how this felt physically and the emotions it engendered, I checked back with the threesome. The women said the young man watched, touched each of them, and then just disappeared. They were concerned that he had felt rejected in some way.

I found him again leaning against a back wall. I didn't speak but just smiled, reached out and cupped his face tenderly. Within seconds, tears began running down his face. A little later he told me that no one had touched him tenderly like that since his mother had died. We talked a few minutes about his need for touch and his avoidance of it because it was so emotional for him. Afterwards, he eagerly participated in the rest of the workshop and left beaming.

This incident illustrates the immense power of touch and its connection with love. In our interpersonal relationships, we demonstrate love by tender, gentle, warm touching. We show love through affirming, encouraging, supporting words, but we *trust* demonstrations of love most when they come through the medium of physical touch.

So, on the one hand, we have a widespread, deep yearning for touch. Unfortunately, our culture places strict limitations on our touching behavior. Our social consciousness limits our touch to socially acceptable and symbolic occasions. Thus, we have a situation where we need touch and where, unless we've been seriously deprived, we enjoy touching and being touched. We trust this channel of communication, yet we find ourselves hooked on the horns of a social dilemma whereby society severely limits this touching behavior.

One area where touching behavior is limited is in public displays of affection. Some people practice it, and others don't. Some onlookers love it, while others see it as disgusting, or at least, inappropriate. With adults, public displays of affection, unless in "legitimate" situations such as greeting and leave-taking, often trigger feelings similar to the reactions of children watching their parents hug and kiss. Because of the intense emotions involved, children will turn away from such a scene or try to break

it up. Adults often react the same way. Affectionate behavior confronts some people with their aloneness, an un-
settling reality at best.

Sometimes onlookers reject public touching because
anything beyond a handshake or a back pat takes on sexual overtones in our society. Sometimes, there *are* sexual
overtones; then onlookers, sensing a marked difference
from a mere affectionate, friendly touch, feel as though
they are standing at an open bedroom door, somewhat
like voyeurs.

Some interesting experiments have been done
throughout the years with respect to these societal restraints. In Chicago some years ago, I participated in an
exercise I've come to refer to as the "camera check." A
group of about 50 strangers, both male and female, milled
about a room with their eyes closed. Occasionally, the
facilitator would yell, "Picture!" and the participants
would respond with a rapid blinking of the eyes as if
opening and closing the shutter of a camera. The exercise
demonstrated how we use our eyes, our vision, to judge
and evaluate, thus acting as social critics. Most of us
reported that we began to feel more and more comfortable until a "camera check" came and we took our pictures
with our blinking eyes.

The use of our eyes for visual and nonverbal cues
inhibited us and changed the feelings of closeness and intimacy that we were beginning to feel for each other.
Then we were told we could not open our eyes for quite
a while and that we ought to use our bodies, hands, and
faces to explore our feelings and the bodies of those
around us. Soon, in my self-imposed darkness, I experienced a yearning, a need to make contact with others.
I began to move around more freely, touching with my

hands and body any other body I came close to. Others essentially reported the same reaction.

Toward the end of the exercise and for quite a while afterward, I felt such an intense need for physical contact it frightened me. In my ignorance, I labeled this feeling sexual desire. I did not know at that time of the hunger for human touch, of "skin hunger," which runs much deeper than a desire for sex.

Another experiment dealing with darkness and touching was conducted at Swarthmore College outside of Philadelphia. Several groups were used in the study, each consisting of eight unacquainted subjects, equally male and female, who were placed one at a time in a 10 x 12 room, with padded walls and ceilings and totally dark except for a tiny red light over the door. The subjects knew they would spend an hour or less in the room with other people and would be escorted from the area alone afterwards. Therefore, they would never meet other participants in the light. They were also told no rules governed what they did together. Infrared cameras and tape recorders were used to observe and listen to the activities. The overall results were that within 30 minutes conversation had almost stopped. Almost 90 percent of the participants touched others. Nearly 50 percent hugged another person, and 80 percent reported being sexually aroused. Many kissed and "loved" one another.

In that darkened room with anonymous strangers there were many behavior alternatives, yet almost all of the participants shed the usual societal restraints and inhibitions and chose to touch, to be close and affectionate, to hug and cuddle, to stroke and fondle rather than communicate with words.

Most of us would agree that love is the compelling

force behind life. When we don't have love, we desperately search for it or bemoan the fact that it's slipped through our fingers again. Yet, we withhold a part of love that is the most trusted, the most satisfying, the most fulfilling to another human being. We close ourselves off; we keep our hands and our bodies to ourselves. Except for certain socially acceptable or very private times, we adopt a policy of "folded arms" rather than outstretched, welcoming ones. We find touching extremely difficult even if we recognize the enormous need for it, or if we do touch, it is in unfulfilling ways. This may be because touch is so straightforward, honest and unambiguous.

If someone hugs or strokes you, you know how the giver feels about you. This is one area where we cannot easily hide the truth about what we feel. The exchange of words can be clouded in nuances, shaded in ambiguities, seeming to mean one thing, yet really suggesting something far different. Touch cannot. Touch speaks directly to the heart.

One day, I was discussing the honesty of touch with my InterPersonal Communication class (I.P.C.) when one young man, a high school senior, took issue with what I was saying. He argued that if someone was touched on a nonsexual area of the body, there was no way to know if the touch was caring or sexual in intent.

I reached out and touched his forearm with my fingertips. "You mean with a touch like this, you couldn't be sure of the message?" I asked. "Well, I know you care about me, so I know what the touch means," he replied. I closed my eyes for a few seconds to remember the last time I'd made mad passionate love and captured one moment of sheer animal lust! Then I reached out and again touched his forearm with my fingertips. He jumped as if I'd applied an electric current to his skin. He looked at me in amazement. "Aha," I said. "You *do* know the difference, even coming from someone you wouldn't expect it from!"

Although young children might not be able to differentiate between different forms of touch they do know what feels good and what feels bad, it is as we mature we learn the difference between a warm, *caring* touch, a *healing* touch and a *sexual* touch. We may choose to ignore the subtleties of each kind of touch, but we really do know. We can discriminate. Sometimes, we try to kid ourselves about being close to someone, loving them. But if we can't lovingly, physically touch them, are we actually close? Do we truly love them?

Because of the power of touch, because it is such a persuasive form of communication, it hurts me to think that so many children grow up equating touching with anger or pain. When we stop loving or when we withhold our love, as in anger or punishment, we often convey our feelings through touch or nontouch.

Touch can communicate more love in five seconds than words can in five minutes. Hugging someone who is having a bad day can be more healing than all the words of support we could possibly utter. Greeting someone with a warm embrace meaningfully says, "I'm really glad to see you."

As part of the loving process, touching is natural and healthy in human beings. Indeed, it is necessary for health, both emotional and physical. Researchers believe it builds our sense of self-esteem. When we stop extending our love and our touch for any reason, we begin to jeopardize not only the well-being of others, but of ourselves. We cannot lose by touching lovingly; we can only gain. Even if some people don't accept our touch, others will gladly receive it. Let us choose to hone this wonderful ability of ours by reaching out to touch those we care about, those we love, thereby drawing to ourselves the affection, warm feelings, and physical attention we need.

Imagine a child describing the role of touch in her feelings of being loved:

> *My parents talk, touch and kiss me all the time. When my mother brushes my hair and braids it, she enjoys doing it. Before my father tucks me in at night, he rubs my back, and I feel as though my skin were the most wondrous material in the world. Though I'm getting pretty big, I still get to be rocked in the big "grandma's" chair. I can't wait to come home from school to get my afternoon hugging.*

Contrast this description with what you know and observe of how children are actually touched or not touched. In one group, after I had spent several evenings discussing touching and doing touch activities, Dan, a divorced father of three little girls, shared an experience. It seems he dreaded the weekends he had "visitation." He said that his little girls drove him crazy. They hung all over him, whined, cried, wouldn't go to sleep at night, wouldn't eat their hamburgers, and so on.

Then he began to look at the situation in terms of skin hunger. When he picked the girls up, he made a point of giving each a long, close hug. He carried them around when they went places, giving each their turn. He rocked them in his arms, and and at night he made sure that each child had a back rub before lights-out. Dan was amazed at the difference in his children. Moreover he found he was looking forward to being with them. He was meeting his own needs, too.

Dan's children acted out in reaction to unmet needs, however, this is not always the case. In my I.P.C. class, one project was to recall and write about a childhood fantasy. An excerpt from Martin's essay illustrates another method for coping with unmet touching needs. He wrote the following:

> *From about the age of six until thirteen, I would fantasize myself to sleep. I would lie on my back drifting to a world totally separate from reality. My fantasy was situated within a hospital. It was staffed with the heroes of the television shows I watched, mostly female. I had some strange and undiagnosable disease that had no ill side effects but with the stipulation on treatment being that I underwent a rigid schedule each day of total body massages. It was in the middle of many of these physical massages that I fell asleep. The intense thinking required to maintain this fantasy state also allowed for my body to really believe it was happening. The relaxation lulled me to sleep . . . .my body would tingle as the hands ran over my limbs. I had always loved when my mother had scratched my back as a small child, and I somehow believe this contributed heavily to this fantasy.*
>
> *I have no theories pertaining to why it was in the hospital. It was perhaps the only environment in which my mind could rationalize touching to such an extent. I do know that* lack of touching *weighed heavily on my*

strong desire for touch. Now as my mind functions on a more rational level, it is difficult to convince myself of such a fantasy. But the endless nights I used this technique led to the person I am today. If nothing else, I gained the compassion and understanding of what touch can do if used correctly. It helped one kid overcome some turbulent years—childhood.

It is my fervent hope that with enough information about the need for touch, particularly for children, that more experiences such as Dan's discovery of the effects of touch occur and that fantasies such as Mark's are no longer necessary, especially not in well-educated, middle class families such as Martin grew up in. By focusing on particular subjects, students heightened their awareness in different areas. Shakespeare compared the world to a stage and the people in it to actors. In this context, one of the many reasons I so enjoyed working with high school students was that they were still open. They were still in the process of writing their scripts before their play went on the road. Societal inhibitions and restraints, especially about touch, weren't yet set in concrete for them. They were open to exploring and learning and changing.

In I.P.C., after we discussed touching and the need for it in our lives, students began to drop by my room before school, after school, and in emergencies, during school. Often the only comment was, "I need a hug. I'm having a terrible day!" Sometimes my sophomore English class would be in session. Not one of these younger students ever questioned these interruptions yet an interesting phenomenon occurred. Almost every time I sat down at my desk, one, two, sometimes more students would cluster closely around me with the pretext of some question. They stayed until I had touched them in some way— on the hand, on the arm, a pat on the back, or sometimes on the cheek. I don't believe they consciously knew that they were responding to their own need. I decided touching must be contagious. What a wonderful virus it is!

I left teaching in 1980 but have returned to the high school where I taught to speak to I.P.C. classes several times. After one such occasion, I received a letter, one of many, that ended with this paragraph:

> *Touching is very important in all of our lives. Now I understand why when I was with my boyfriend (we've just recently broken up) I felt so loved. It seems when we were together, just holding hands, it gave me a warm, secure feeling. I just wanted to thank you for coming and for touching the most important part of a person—her heart.*
>
> *Thank you,*
> *Barbara*

There are many ways of loving and relating to people. There are also many barriers in the form of social consciousness to our freedom of expression. May this book help you open your heart and your mind. For, from the heart comes love, and from love the touching flows naturally.

To all the I.P.C. students from whom I have learned, and whom I have touched in some way, to those whom I taught who touched me in so many loving ways, I dedicate this poem . . .

PLEASE TOUCH ME

If I am your baby,
Please touch me.
I need your touch in ways you may never know.
Don't just wash and diaper and feed me,
But rock me close, kiss my face and stroke my body.
Your soothing, gentle touch says security and love.

If I am your child,
Please touch me.
Though I may resist, even push you away,
Persist, find ways to meet my needs.
Your goodnight hug helps sweeten my dreams.
Your daytime touching tells me how you really feel.

If I am your teenager,
Please touch me.
Don't think because I'm almost grown,
I don't need to know that you still care.
I need your loving arms, I need a tender voice.
When the road gets rocky, then the child in me still needs.

If I am your friend,
Please touch me.
Nothing lets me know you care like a warm embrace.
A healing touch when I'm depressed assures me I am
    loved,
And reassures me that I am not alone.
Yours may be the only comforting touch I get.

If I am your sexual partner,
Please touch me.
You may think that your passion is enough,
But only your arms hold back my fears.
I need your tender reassuring touch,
To remind me I am loved just because I am me.

If I am your grown-up child,
Please touch me.
Though I may have a family of my own to hold,
I still need Mommy's, Daddy's arms when I hurt.
As a parent the view is different,
I appreciate you more.

If I am your aging parent,
Please touch me.
The way I was touched when I was very young.
Hold my hand, sit close to me, give me strength,
And warm my tired body with your nearness.
Although my skin is worn wrinkled, it loves to be
        stroked.

Don't be afraid.
Just touch me.

2 ○ The Sense of Touch

Our touch sense gives us our knowledge of depth or thickness and form; we feel, we love and hate, are "touchy" and are touched through the touch corpuscles of our skin.

 To speak of touch is to speak of skin. Our skin which covers us like a giant envelope, is an organ that receives tactile, or sensory, impressions and responds to any contact with specific sensations. Skin receptors respond to warmth, cold, touch, itchiness, ticklishness, types of pain and vibration. The skin, the largest organ of our body, comprises 15 to 20 percent of our body weight. The average human body has 18 square feet of skin dotted with approximately five million tiny nerve endings acting as transmitters of sensations.

The skin is the most important organ, next to the brain. The tactile areas of the brain cover a surprisingly large area, both in the sensory and motor regions. The lips, tongue, face, thumb, fingers, and hands take up a disproportionate amount of cerebral space, followed closely by the feet. The diagram on the next page illustrates the largest tactile areas represented in the brain. Notice particularly the lips and tongue, and the hand. If you were

17

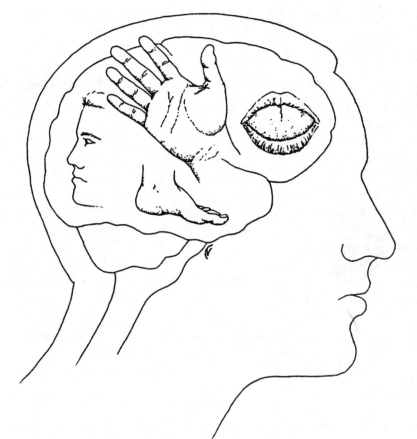

THE MOST SENSITIVE TACTILE AREAS
REPRESENTED IN THE BRAIN

to brush your fingertips across your lips, run your hands over your nose and face, and lick your lips with your tongue, you would stimulate the most sensitive areas of your body. Our sense of touch is very dominant in our fingers and hands.

Through our skin we are constantly involved with what goes on outside us. Unless we turn our awareness to our skin, we remain generally unconscious of our highly complex and significant tactile experiences. Right now, if you are sitting, become aware of the pressure of the chair against your buttocks and back, the feeling of the floor beneath your feet. Tune into the contact caused by crossed legs or perhaps fingertips touching your face or body, the sensations of the hands holding this book. Sense the temperature of your skin and any air currents gently whispering around your face or other exposed areas. Be aware of any other surface skin sensations such as itching.

Note the space between clothing and skin, where it is loose and where it is restricting. Perhaps, feel the weight of glasses on your nose, the impression of jewelry on your skin, the sense of hair (or absence of hair) on your head. Become conscious of any slight movement of your lips or tongue as you read. Air pressure, wind, sunlight, sound waves, vibrations and sometimes even other human beings likewise impinge upon us through our skin, whether we consciously notice them or not.

When we are very young, we pay little attention to our skin, not even caring if it is dirty or oily or freckled. During adolescence we begin to care about these matters and often bemoan the existence of pimples and other blemishes. As we age, we scrutinize our skins for signs of betrayal. We may notice that with the passing years, our skin envelope ceases to fit as snugly and smoothly. It crinkles and sags and bags and dries. I sometimes wonder whether our skin would wear completely out if we lived long enough! But, regardless of age, our skin reacts sensitively to the outside world.

The sensitivity of our skin can become a major health problem. Fifty percent of workers' compensation claims relate to chronic skin disorders. Seven million new patients seek medical attention for skin problems every year according to a 1982 U.S. Department of Health survey. The survey also reports that three million people lose work days every year due to skin problems. Whatever the underlying cause, emotional problems increase the severity and frequency of skin disorders. It seems that the human skin becomes a symbolic outlet for inner emotional problems, for repressed emotions. The idea that the skin is a voice for inner emotional problems is over one hundred years old. "Neurodermatitis", a word coined by two French doctors, Brocq and Jacquet, in 1891, describes skin inflammations resulting from emotional states.

A 1978 study of almost 5,000 patients by dermatologist Robert Grieshmer found that emotions are clearly the instigator in many cases. Specifically, 27 percent of cysts were triggered by underlying emotional problems, as were colds and shingles at 36 percent; psoriasis, 62 percent; hives, 68 percent; eczema, ranging from 56 to 70 percent; itching, 86 percent; warts, 95 percent; severe scratching and subsequent tearing of skin, 98 percent; and profuse sweating was 100 percent psychologically caused. In an attempt to help with psychological problems, the skin produces symptoms to call attention to this inner cry for release. Unfortunately, when they are unheeded these signals manifest themselves as unsightly or painful skin conditions. Help for these emotionally linked skin problems is available in various ways and is discussed in the chapter on healing touch.

When our skin receives sensory impressions and responds to any contact, it is with the sensation of touch. The touch sensation occurs as a result of the most minute contact and activates the appropriate nerve endings, which relay sensory messages along the spinal column to the brain. The earliest, most elemental, and possibly the most dominant experience of the unborn baby is the tactile experience.

Human meaning becomes associated with touch from the moment of birth and continues throughout our life. Although touching, or tactile stimulation, has received relatively little attention as compared to our other senses and modes of communication, it remains the most basic form of communication and subconsciously we know it. Even our language speaks of touch. We use many "touching" expressions.

- We "rub" people the wrong way.
- Someone may be a "soft" touch.
- People "get in touch."
- Some people must be "handled with kid gloves."
- Other people are "thick-skinned" or "thin-skinned."
- Things get "under our skin."
- A deeply felt experience is "touching."
- Something superficial is only "skin deep."
- Our society has been called "touch-starved."

You can probably add many more expressions to the list. Listen for "touching" expressions as people talk. Right now, think of any words or phrases you use or remember others using associated with the skin or touching.

Can you now understand why touch is fundamental to the development of human behavior? It is a basic need, which must be satisfied for an organism to survive. As human beings, our needs include:

- Food,
- Water,
- Oxygen,
- Rest,
- Activity,
- Sleep,
- Bowel and bladder elimination,
- Protection from danger,
- Avoidance of pain and,
- SKIN STIMULATION!

Notice that sex is not included, since a person's survival does not depend on sexual gratification. However, *skin stimulation* through touch is a basic need.

I would define *touch* specifically as the satisfying feeling of skin-to-skin contact. Touching can be soothing, healing, caring, affectionate, comforting, or reassuring. It may take the form of stroking, patting, massaging, caressing, cuddling, hugging, or holding. It may vary from a brief brush to the massive tactile stimulation of sexual intercourse. Our touch sense gives us our knowledge of depth or thickness and form. We attach our own meanings to touch. Each of us, as do cultures, vary in the way we express the need for touch and the way in which we attempt to satisfy it.

As we develop through infancy, touch becomes associated with feelings; thus, touch becomes an emotional occurrence. Touch itself is not an emotional occurrence, but its sensory elements produce neural, glandular, muscular, and mental changes that we then refer to as emotions. This concept is important to understand because we attach emotions and meanings to touch as a result of the manner in which emotions and meanings were conveyed to us through touch in our childhood. If we experience affection and involvement through touch, then touch will come to mean affection and involvement to us. It will also come to represent security. We feel, we love and hate, we touch and are touched through the touch corpuscles of our skin.

Even though this attachment of emotions and meanings to touch occurred in childhood, to believe that our childhood learnings and associations cannot be rechanneled or changed is unduly pessimistic. Energy, willingness, patience, and reexamination of our beliefs can work wonders. True, touch can be frightening. It reveals so much about us; it touches us so deeply. It is no accident that we refer to both physical touch and emotion with the same word—FEELING.

The sense of touching and of being touched is highly developed in some of us, while others have a relative insensitivity to touch, have a heavy touch, or even have an avoidance to touch. The more we use our sense of touch, the more it develops. For instance, blind people develop great sensitivity to outward occurrences through their skin, especially their fingertips. Some can even distinguish colors with their touch. My chiropractor says the touch corpuscles in his fingertips have become so sensitive that he finds it painful to tap his fingertips firmly on a hard surface. In workshops, or on your own, you can learn to develop more sensitivity to touching and being touched.

The potency of the act of touching another person, even for less than a second, is striking. It can make people feel better and even begin to associate these good feelings with other stimuli. For example, Heslin, Rytting, and Fisher conducted experiments with touch at Purdue University. Library clerks were asked to touch some borrowers on their hands and not touch others when they presented their library cards. Questioned immediately afterward, those who were touched briefly, even those who were unaware of the touch, had more positive feelings about themselves, the library, and the clerks who helped them.

Another time, Heslin asked a student to leave a dime in a public telephone booth. The student would leave the booth and then approach the person who entered immediately afterward. Each time she asked if the dime she had left had been found. The answer was almost always no. Then the student tried another approach. She gently touched each person on his or her arm for a few seconds as she asked. Using this method, she got the dime back almost every time.

We can learn to eliminate the confusion so widespread regarding touch. We can learn to distinguish between a perfunctory touch and a passionate touch. Maybe you already know that. Have you been kissed, patted, or hugged by someone you either didn't know or didn't share friendly feelings with? That is a perfunctory touch. It is casual, superficial. The people doing it are not really concerned with you as a person. They are indifferent to your feelings. They are simply engaging in a social act.

Then again, if you have been touched by someone who is amorous, desirous of sexual contact, whose very touch seems full of heat, you know the passionate touch. It is intense, deeply emotional and concerned with arousing this same passion in you and your body. But, you *can* learn to distinguish between a healing, comforting, soothing touch, a caring, friendly touch, and a touch for sexual arousal if you cannot already tell the difference. By so doing you remove one more touching restraint. Remember the student in chapter one who asserted the impossibility of distinguishing between kinds of touch?

The following similar exercise astounds many people. When I explain it to a group, invariably someone will say, "But I don't think I can tell the difference." Sometimes we repeat the exercise several times until everyone gets the "feel" of it.

EMOTIONAL TOUCH
DISCRIMINATION EXERCISE

Sit facing your partner, closely enough so you can comfortably reach his or her forearm with your hand. You will be touching your partner four times by using your hand and fingertips on his or her forearm. The primary difference with each touch will result from what you think and feel as you touch. Tell your partner you intend to convey anger, tenderness, noninvolvement and sexual desire. Spend enough time to really think, imagine and feel these emotions before you touch your partner. As soon as the receiver experiences each touch, he or she should tell you what that touch seems to represent. Do not confirm or deny the impression until you have completed all four touches.

To begin, the receiver closes his or her eyes and waits. Then you touch, with emphasis on each emotion, allowing enough time in between for you to prepare yourself for the next touch and for the receiver to tell what he or she thinks the touch represented.

Try envisioning the following to establish each emotion within yourself before touching.

TENDERNESS: Imagine touching a sick child, a beloved pet, or someone you feel protective or very loving toward. The touch should be gentle, delicate, soft.

ANGER: Imagine being angry, really ticked off at someone, as if you'd like to let them have it, really boiling and fuming. The touch should be quick, hard, and unpleasurable.

DETACHMENT: In your head, multiply 495 X 3 and divide the answer by 2. Touch lightly while you mentally do the math problem.

SEXUALITY: Imagine your wildest fantasy, and when you get to an arousing or exciting part, imagine an electric current emanating from your hands and fingertips, then touch the receiver.

After all four responses, let the receiver know what order you used for the touches. If he or she got less than two correct, you might want to repeat it later.

Now switch places so the receiver gives the touches

in any order, and you receive and respond. **Repeat the exercise.**

Touch communicates without words. We can tell the difference between kinds of touches. We can say "no" if a touch is inappropriate or not what we want at that particular moment. And most importantly, we can learn to touch with awareness, respect, and tenderness.

Touch becomes a physical expression of our attitude toward the world. Do you reach out for it, passively welcome it, wait to receive it, resist it with folded arms, or avoid it altogether? Do you find it pleasing, frightening, or challenging to touch and be touched?

We aren't babies anymore. We can give and receive love in ways other than by physical touching, but touching is a gauge of how we are able to love. We need touch for its own sake; we also need touch to keep us honest. We are skilled in lying to ourselves about our feelings and our motives. Touch is tangible, and you can't fake an emotion when touching someone unless that person wants to be fooled. You can't give a perfunctory touch while saying you care or a sexual touch while saying you just want to be friends and make it believable. You will know the difference, and so will the one you touch. Touch symbolizes how you relate to life, to experience, to friendship, and to love. Take a few minutes now to think of several words or phrases that describe and characterize your present approach toward touching. Also, think of several words or phrases that you would *like* to have describe and characterize your approach to touching.

The sense of touch resides in our skin and in our brain. Feeling refers to both physical touch and emotion. Our skin weeps with despair, itches with frustration, erupts in anger as it reacts with sensitivity to both our inner and our outer experiences. We learn to communicate through touch, and it remains our basic communication mode throughout our life. We need skin stimulation to survive, and touch is a satisfying way to obtain it. Touch can be powerful, loving, and also frightening because of emotions and meanings we attached to touch as children. Touch is such an integral, necessary, and joyous potentiality that we must learn to use it fully, honestly, and lovingly. We can begin by eliminating any confusion between different kinds of touches.

3 ○ The Need for Touch in Infancy

Touch is not a pleasant stimulus but a biological necessity.

Each of us arrives into the world with various needs. One of these is the need for touch. This may be referred to as tactile stimulation, body contact, physical contact, tactual sensitivity, or skin hunger. Whatever the label we give to touch and regardless of how much the intensity of the touch varies, the need remains. Touch is not a pleasant stimulus but a biological necessity. During the nine months the fetus grows in the womb, its skin is constantly stimulated by rhythmic impacts transmitted through and magnified by amniotic fluid. So the fetus has its first experience with tactile stimulation even before its emergence into the world. At birth, the soft rocking movements stop as uterine contractions intensify the tactile experience until birth occurs.

These uterine contractions serve as the initial caressing or skin stimulation of the infant. These uterine hugs stimulate nerves in the infant's skin. Being born actually provides a massage that vitalizes the emerging infant—a way of stimulation that should be continued immediately for a considerable time after birth. However, at this point, the infant is only briefly handled for cleaning, wrapping, and weighing. Sometimes, as was customary in the past, the doctor holds the infant upside down and spanks it. Then, as is still often the custom in our country, the infant is relegated to a room and placed in one of a line of cribs. The soft rocking movements, the warm security of Mother's body, and the tactile stimulation abruptly cease at a time the infant still needs them. There the infant lies until setting up a howl of protest or until feeding time. However, the infant really needs parent or parents to immediately establish skin-to-skin contact with him to reaffirm a sense of safety and security.

Studies show that premature or cesarean section babies run a greater risk of developmental problems and require regular concentrated period of hugging, rocking, and stroking after birth, perhaps to replace what they missed in prebirth "hugs."

Researchers working with monkeys, rats, goats, chickens, and other animals believe that the face-to-face and skin-to-skin contact between mother and child creates maternal affection and binds the two together. If this touching and face-to-face contact decreases, so does the strength of the affection.

Goats show how nature provides for the affectional bond. In experiments, kids were removed from the mother goats five to ten minutes following birth for periods of thirty minutes to an hour. Thereafter, the mother goats seemed unable to identify their offspring from others and exhibited rejecting behavior.

Pediatricians Marshall Klaus and John Kennell proposed in a 1976 book, *Maternal-Infant Bonding*, that something similar occurs when human babies are born. They called this *"bonding"* to refer to the emotional link. Although, in a new 1982 edition retitled *Parent-Infant Bonding*, they somewhat modified their stance due to controversy, their theory raises an interesting point. In an interview with Jane Brody of the New York Times, Dr. Klaus said, "Right now, there are no studies that confirm or deny the presence of a sensitive period or that measure how much contact is needed between mother and baby during the first hours or days of life to have an effect."

The original theory proposed that the mother-infant bond in the first hours or days improved mothering, increased the likelihood of breastfeeding, enhanced child development, and prevented child abuse and neglect. Some researchers challenged this by saying that if the early contact affects how well a mother cares for her baby, the effect is small and limited to some mothers under some circumstances.

However, it is difficult, if not impossible, in studies of human behavior, to establish tight scientific controls and to measure and interpret human responses. These same critics do, however, approve of changes in hospital practices such as allowing early contact when parents want it and allowing fathers into the delivery room. In other words, treating the birthing process as an emotional and social activity, not an illness. One of the problems cited by critics with the "bonding period" theory is the prompting of feelings of guilt and fear of failure in parents who missed this period or in mothers who, exhausted or preferring to be alone, do not choose to have the infants with them. "Unfortunately," says Dr. Klaus, "the word bonding has become confused with epoxy glue," which is too literal an interpretation! Because the work has been misinterpreted doesn't mean it is invalid.

The main issue here does not seem to be the bonding process, although that is certainly important, but instead, the early physical contact written about by anthropologist, Ashley Montague. I highly recommend his very detailed and research-oriented 1971 book, *Touching: The Human Significance of the Skin,* for those of you wanting to read more on the subject.

Another argument for increased early physical contact between mother and child comes from the study of animals. In some animals, removal of the young immediately after birth seriously retards the recovery of the mothers. Nuzzling, licking, nursing, and other physical contact not only creates an affectional bond, but aids in physical recovery. This could explain why in many more primitive countries women seem to recover from childbirth more quickly than in our "scientific," but in many ways inhumane, hospitals. The physical contact that is immediately established and then continued stimulates the mother's body to resume its prebirth condition. If you have been a mother who breastfed her baby, then you are familiar with the uterine contractions experienced while nursing. In primitive countries, such mothers not only nurse their children on demand, but they carry them close to their body, often with bare skin touching bare skin.

Now, where men are concerned, it seems that when fathers have physical contact with their babies soon after birth, several benefits occur. Fathers feel more involved with and closer to the baby as well as less left out of the birthing process. Surely, this would have a great effect on later care, affection, and touching of their child.

There can be no doubt that in infancy there is a biological need for touch. All mammal young demonstrate the necessity of touch to healthy physical and behavioral development. Even baby rats prosper from being handled and petted. When they are touched and handled, they out-weigh, outlearn, and outlive other rats.

Early in the nineteenth century, over one-half of infants died during the first year of life. The disease was named *marasmus*, a Greek word meaning "wasting away." In the United States, less than fifty years ago, infant mortality was almost one hundred percent for infants under one year of age being raised in orphanages. At that time the recommended child-rearing procedure was based on the advice published in the *Care and Feeding of Children* by Dr. Holt in 1894. Eliminate the cradle, don't pick the baby up when it cries, feed it only by the clock, and prevent "spoiling" by undue handling except for necessary cleaning and feeding were some of Dr. Holt's suggestions. In 1935, the publication was in its fifteenth edition and government pamphlets in the 1960's *still* recommended the same thing! These dogmatic teachings have persisted, and even now, some doctors and parents subscribe to this "scientific" child-rearing procedure.

Recently, as I counseled a couple with a young child, one conflict that emerged revolved around the wife picking up their baby when it cried. It cried a lot, and the husband contended that the child cried because it was "spoiled" by the wife's behavior. The mother didn't question the word spoiled but defended her actions by saying that perhaps the baby had colic. The word *spoil* has several meanings, I told them. One is to impair the disposition by overindulgence. Another is to impair seriously; to mar; to ruin. It seemed farfetched to me to think that a four-month-old child, whose mother works and whose father doesn't like to "fool around" with babies, could be overindulged. Impaired by lack of holding, cuddling, and rocking, yes. *Spoiled* but not in the sense that Dr. Holt meant.

My second child was born in 1962. The pediatrician warned that his advice to me was not exactly traditional, however, it seemed to work. He told me that a schedule would be strictly for the family's convenience, not the baby's. I could attempt to establish one, but if my new son cried between specified times not to worry if I fed or cuddled him. Wonderful! I thought. I could do what I'd already done with my first child and not feel guilty about it! He said babies don't spoil. That made sense to me. Babies don't think much; they aren't Machiavellian. Babies just respond, usually by crying in response to their biological needs. The only unfortunate aspect of this method is that babies' needs often conflict with parents' needs, such as the need to sleep. A helpful father and willing relatives can help satisfy everyone's needs.

Almost everyone has heard of TLC. TLC, or *Tender Loving Care*, was a revolutionary idea brought to America by a Boston doctor, Fritz Talbot, who observed a children's clinic in Germany before World War I. There, he discovered a woman named Anna. Anna was old and fat and shuffled around. She seemed to do nothing but carry babies around with her. Yet, by doing so she literally saved many a baby's life.

It wasn't until after World War II, however, that studies were done investigating the cause of marasmus, or unexplained infant death, and a link was established with respect to lack of touch. Infant mortality rates declined dramatically in those places where TLC was applied. In order to survive and develop healthfully, a child needs to be carried, cuddled, caressed, and "cooed" to as old Anna did. This would in no way establish a tyranny of the child, but rather it would meet a basic need in the early years of a child's life.

Case histories abound of children who make miraculous recoveries simply by the application of TLC. Many years ago, I heard the story of Susan. When Susan was a baby, her mother complained that the child didn't like to be held. Eventually she got tired of trying to hold her and stopped. I don't know about Susan's mother, but often mothers communicate their own anxiety and stress to their babies, who then cry a lot when held. Another explanation is that Susan was a baby who intensely resisted restraint in any form—not touching but the way in which touching might have been given. Irregardless of the reason Susan resisted holding, so her mother stopped. Finally, when at 22 months old, Susan weighed only 15 pounds, closer to the weight of an average six-month-old, she was taken to a hospital. Doctors could find no physical reason for her lack of motor skills, inability to speak, and fear of people. After only two months at the hospital, the young girl openly showed affection and began improving in the areas in which she was once deficient. The miracle, so it seemed, wasn't due to medical care or a fantastic drug. Susan was cured by a medicine known as touching.

Nurturing parents can meet some of the touch needs of infants by the everyday routine of feeding, burping, bathing, powdering, holding, and caressing. Some, not all. Have you ever watched a mother dog licking and nuzzling her puppies? The stimulation is continual in the beginning. I observed our collie named Gentle, with her puppies. As soon as she finished licking and nuzzling one, she started on another. With six puppies, that took most of her time. Time in our society seems to be something we don't have enough of. Or maybe it is our sense of priorities. Propping the bottle doesn't provide for touching needs;

neither does cleaning house, cooking, working, and so on. But as many mothers exclaim, "All those things *have* to be done!"

Maybe a solution is to do things differently. Priorities need to be carefully established and examined. Motherhood needs to be recognized and provided for in more ways than simply finding child care so the mother can go back to work. I realize that in some cases economics force both parents to work. In other cases, however, it is not necessity, but simply the desire for a certain standard of living. Each individual couple must find their own solution.

Solutions could range from delaying parenthood until a certain amount of money is saved to enable one parent to stay home for at least the first year. Or one of the parents could work only part-time for a while if the income is needed. Another alternative might be a live-in grandparent or whatever can help balance the need of the nurturing that the child needs and the needs of the parents. Even if the mother, or as has been done in some cases, the father, stays home for the first year, that nurturing parent also needs lot of help and understanding in devoting enough time to the baby to satisfy its needs.

In third-world countries, babies are in constant physical contact with the mother's body by some type of sling or carrying device worn by the mother. Father could share this activity, also. It would not only help the baby, but the father as well. Both parents can develop a sense of contributing to the baby's physical and emotional growth if they will share the carrying of the baby for the first year or so.

A baby learns about love and touching by being loved and touched. Bringing a baby home from the hospital in a plastic carrier and putting it in a stationary crib at home doesn't convey loving or touching. The long periods of stillness and silence don't stimulate it. Where is the warmth of loving arms, the gentle rocking movement, the safety and security the baby has had for nine months?

The results of two recent research studies are pertinent here. One new theory says that babies don't distinguish between their sensory systems of hearing, vision, and touch. In other words, all sensory input is as one. One sensory experience can trigger perception in another. A baby, hearing a sound in a dark room, will reach out and try to grab it. Not until about six months do the senses of vision, hearing, and touching become separate. This particular mode of skill acquisition seems to suggest that rather than innate differences between left and right hemispheres of the brain, which results in a division of activities, the activities themselves cause the specialization of the two hemispheres. In short, the nature of human intelligence may depend on how a baby's sensory systems develop and are stimulated. Stimulating a child's sensory systems actually increases its general alertness and responsiveness to learning. So touching and tactile stimulation can increase a child's intelligence and learning ability.

The second research study shows that benefits to the equilibrium center of the brain occur when a baby is in motion. Movement is essential for infants, particularly when combined with touching. The rocking or touching of a baby directs impulses to the specific part of the brain that stimulates development. This motion and subsequent beneficial development process continues until at least two years of age.

Harry Harlow, in experiments with monkeys reared

with motionless cloth mothers, demonstrated social isolation effects. Because the surrogate mothers did not move, the little monkeys did instead, in repetitive rocking motions. If cloth surrogate mothers were used that moved, then the young monkeys didn't. This is another illustration of the need for rocking motions for babies. Infants, children, and adults who have been immobilized for fracture treatment, illness, or experimental reasons develop emotional disturbances ranging from rage and violence to bizarre thoughts, hyperactivity, intellectual inefficiency, and unusual body sensations. Note, the only sense restricted was movement. Vision and hearing remained undisturbed.

Touching does other things for a child. As the child begins to differentiate between himself and the world around him, he expands his knowledge through being touched, touching objects and exploring his own body. Children learn spatial dimensions, sizes, shapes, textures, pleasure, and love through touch and manipulation of things. A baby's brain grows to seventy percent of its adult weight in the first year of life. Babies react to the world through their senses. By stimulating their sense of touch, you stimulate the brain.

Through touching his own body, a child contributes to his own body image. This self-exploration couples with how the body feels and the reactions of others to this exploration. A child who has painful bowel movements, constipation, or is treated roughly or berated for bowel movements—in or out of diapers or pants—adopts a negative attitude toward that part of his body and that biological function. I, and many with me, shudder to think of how I potty-trained my children in my ignorance. Think of the numerous hang-ups we Americans have about our bodies and their normal functions! Pleasurable or painful tactile experiences, then, reinforce the body image.

Parents who discourage body exploration and self-touching in their child desperately need to be educated. They cut off an important part of perceptual learning and encourage a negative attitude toward their child's body. This physical contact gives the child a strong sense of psychological security, reassurance, comfort, and well-being. Touching helps overcome fear and a sense of isolation. The child who is encouraged or allowed to touch his own body and who receives a positive response when touching others should develop positive feelings about the human body and his own body in particular.

If a baby is limited in tactile experiences, denied sufficient opportunities to receive or send touching communication, then he must wait for sufficient development of his visual and auditory recognition before he can communicate with others. In addition, he must learn through experiences prescribed by others and becomes more dependent than other children upon the authority of his parents. A submissive, compliant child may seem desirable at times, but he will not be a happy, well-adjusted adult. Babies whose cries are consistently responded to by touching and rocking are more autonomous by age three than are those babies who are left to cry. Some explanations of why babies might be left to cry are that this non-response might "teach" them independence and that needs of other's are more important than theirs. Heaven forbid that a baby might be dependent or selfish seems to be the idea here.

At no point as the child grows and develops is touch replaced as the basic means of intimate communication. Rather, other forms of communication merely *supplement* touch. Facial expressions and gestures carry their own meanings, and voice begins to form recognizable words.

As I said earlier, in the beginning an infant doesn't distinguish between sounds, touch, and what he sees. At first if the parent holds and cuddles the infant while singing, humming, or talking, later the child will recognize the parent's voice. Still later he will accept it as substitute for actual touch. Thus, where once a child hurried to his parents for holding and reassurance, he will begin to accept their voices saying reassuring words from another room. Similarly, if a child has been spanked, then later a harsh voice and words can produce the same effect on a child.

If we do not receive adequate touching as children the effects are serious. Touching deprivation can cause mental and physical retardation. It has been said by many that we are all a little retarded because none of us received sufficient touching. Some children, in an unconscious effort to secure the touch they need, will deliberately provoke spankings or other physical punishment.

If you have a child with learning or behavioral problems and you have reason to believe that lack of touching and movement is involved, consider the possibility of sensory integration therapy. At the very least, find a therapist who will objectively and caringly apply tactile stimulation to your child.

Since tactile stimulation is such an overwhelming biological requirement, optimally most touching would occur in the first year. Not so in our American society. Children from fourteen months to two years receive more touching than they did as infants. Furthermore, and equally sad, girl babies tend to receive more affectionate touching than do boy babies *after the first six months of life*. Could this partially explain later male attitudes toward touching and explain the seemingly more overt physical need for touching in females?

Girls are also encouraged to spend more time touching and staying close to their parents for a longer period of time. Some may choose to argue that this results from the child's needs, but observation indicates that it is, instead, a result of parental treatment and cultural norms.

The lamentable thing about all this is that, unlike the primate mother or human mothers in other cultures, American parents omit the early phase of close and *constant* physical contact. Since our society passes behaviors and values from one generation to another, it should come as no surprise that this pattern of behavior remains unbroken. If as an infant and child we didn't experience much tactile stimulation, we are reinforced in the lack of touching our own children, and, as an extension, other people we are close to.

In conclusion, being born (unless by cesarean delivery) is a touching massage that vitalizes the emerging infant, a way of stimulation that should be continued immediately after birth and for a considerable time later, for touch is not only a pleasant stimulus but a biological necessity. Studies show the value of tactile stimulation through touching, rocking, stroking, cuddling, washing, and self-stimulation for developing affectional ties and healthy physical and behavioral development of the child. Dogmatic and "scientific" child-rearing advice in the past has contributed to physical, mental, and emotional retardation. American parents omit much of the early biological requirements of close and constant touch, and this pattern of behavior is passed from generation to generation much to the detriment of all.

4 ○ Types of Tactile Stimulation in Infants

Anytime a baby who is well fed, comfortably dry and in no pain cries, he could simply be telling you he needs intimate physical contact. So touch your baby when he cries.

 Realizing that touch in infancy is a biological necessity, it could be interesting to explore the various ways you can provide tactile stimulation for your infant. As far as touching is concerned, the recent controversy of breastfeeding versus bottle feeding is academic. As long as the baby receives adequate skin stimulation, either method is satisfactory. The type of feeding carries far less importance than does the *behavior* of the mother during the process. Cold, reserved mothers who breastfeed have less influence later over their babies than do warm, touching mothers who bottle feed. Babies seem to have a sixth sense about how others feel about them as they are held and touched and respond accordingly. However, the key word here is *satisfactory*. More stimulation is given during breastfeeding to the face and nose, however certain types of nipples are now available that also provide much stimulation. Or, the mother can gently stroke the face and nose while bottle feeding.

For the mother, breastfeeding offers an advantage. For example, a baby allowed to nurse immediately after birth sets up changes in the mother's body. This activity produces uterine contractions which immediately reduce the size of the uterus and help detach the placenta from the uterine wall and eject it.

Various studies cited by Ashley Montagu and the La Leche League demonstrate that breastfed babies are healthier. Breastfed babies have fewer respiratory ailments, diarrhea, eczema, asthma, and other ailments than bottle-fed babies. Additionally, breastfed children tend to be physically and mentally superior in their development, and the longer they are breastfed, the more striking the advances. Evidence indicates that breastfeeding ought to continue for at least a year or longer, until the baby demonstrates a readiness for weaning.

The fact that breastfeeding is advantageous, in other than nutritional ways, does not seem outrageous. First, the mother is, unless unduly pressured into nursing, desirous of close physical contact with her child. Second, with the hand freed that would ordinarily hold a bottle, the mother can engage in more touching, caressing, and general skin stimulation. During breastfeeding experiences, the baby experiences the warmth, odor, and closeness of skin-to-skin contact. It would be interesting to see the results of an experiment in which a baby was bottlefed by some arrangement whereby the mother and baby had skin-to-skin contact and the mother's hand remained easily available for touching.

At a time when women are increasingly becoming

part of the working force due to economic pressures, and at a time when women seek careers and fulfillment as persons rather than as housewives and mothers, many women need to pursue other ways of producing the benefits born of breast-feeding. As suggested earlier, a longer time at home after birth could be advantageous. If the mother has to return to work, then alternating bottle and breast presents a possibility. If bottle fed by both parents, then using skin-to-skin contact between torso and baby and using a bottle holder to completely free the other hand for stroking contributes to tactile stimulation. If necessity dictates leaving the child with a sitter, then make sure the sitter is a warm, caring, touching person and thoroughly explain the biological need for tactile stimulation.

Besides the warmth, odor, and closeness of skin-to-skin contact, another byproduct of the early conditioning of breastfeeding may be in how we treat our noses. Observation shows that people do all sorts of touching to their noses. They stroke, push, flatten, and wrinkle up their noses. One woman, until she met her need for touch in another way, pushed her lip up to touch the smooth underpart of the nose when she felt nervous. Quite possibly, the fact that she had been breastfed and now again, stimulated this area, made her subconsciously feel more secure. Even Santa Claus laid one finger alongside his nose! One explanation of this type of behavior is that it stimulates conditions present when being nursed as an infant. Or perhaps, because of lack of stimulation, the child learned to provide for himself in this manner. From observation, it can be seen that the nose is a favorite part of the body for touching, perhaps because of its prominence and easy

accessibility but definitely because of its large represen-
tation in the tactile area of the brain. How reassuring it
can be to touch and manipulate the nose!

Do an experiment now. With your fingertips, lightly
stroke and caress your nose, especially the smooth under-
side above the lips. Do this with your eyes closed for a few
minutes and observe any thoughts or feelings. Also, watch
how others touch their nose and then check out what you
usually do for your own. It's no wonder that the lips and
mouth become firmly established as erogenous zones. Besides representing a large tactile area in the brain, an infant spends much of his first twelve months of life in
sucking activity. The lips and mouth, consequently, form
the most sensitive contact with the world. The lips,
mouth, tongue, and skin around them are intimately tied
to the sense of smell, vision, and hearing, in addition to
touch.

Another type of tactile stimulation infants receive is
the bathing, powdering and general stimulation of the
genital area. Because the male child's genitalia project ex-
ternally, the penis, scrotum, and gonads are accessible to
more frequent stimulation. It follows that males in all cultures undergo considerably more stimulation and touching in the genital region than do females. Could this
explain the later and greater frequency of masturbation
or self-gratification through skin stimulation in boys than
in girls? Does this have a greater effect on later development and sexual behavior? At this point we can only
speculate.

Many parents believe that pacifiers should not be
used. I've even heard some people comment on how disgusting it looks to see a baby with a pacifier in his mouth
and even impugn a woman's "mothering" ability if her

child is allowed to use one. Despite evidence to the contrary, it has even been suggested that a pacifier causes buck teeth. On the other hand, several studies have suggested that premature babies can benefit by the use of pacifiers. Even though premature infants may be fed through a tube, if they are given pacifiers to suck on during and after tube feeding, they gain weight and become healthier faster than tiny newborns who do not use pacifiers. Even though they consume no more calories than others, they usually gain weight faster. Also, infants given pacifiers progress to bottle feeding sooner than other premature infants and typically go home eight days sooner which would mean a considerable savings on the hospital bill—thousands of dollars, in fact.

Besides pacifiers, other substitutes for or additions to tactile stimulation include thumb-sucking and objects such as rattles, soft stuffed animals, pillows, or blankets. Many children so attach themselves to such objects they are virtually inseparable. One child's "feel piece" (the first time I heard this expression, I didn't know about such security objects and I thought the mother was saying a *field* piece and unless she meant some toy weaponry it made no sense at all) consisted of a two-inch wide by four-foot long strip of blanket. The rest of the blanket had given up the struggle after hundreds of washings! My adult son, Jaye, still has his "doggie"—threadbare, patched in many places, most of the stuffing gone or stiffened—his constant companion for many years. I became a sneak thief in regard to that little stuffed dog. Waiting until he slept soundly, I quietly slipped it from the clasp of his little hands to wash and hopefully dry before he woke up. Sometimes I was successful. Sometimes he hugged to himself a sodden stuffed animal. He didn't seem to care as long as it was there for him. Such objects can be an enormous source of both security and tactile stimulation for young children.

That some parents discourage pacifiers and security objects can only be attributed to ignorance or prejudice. If the child didn't have the need, he wouldn't want such things. If such a need exists then definitely more tactile stimulation such as rocking, touching, and stroking is definitely called for.

Anticipating what some parents might be thinking at this point, I want to tell you that I feel no guilt that I didn't touch my children more. Regret, yes, but how can any of us berate ourselves (or our parents) for lack of knowledge in following what in the past were accepted child care patterns? However, now I would certainly do things differently.

It would be an excellent idea to return the old-fashioned cradle to every home with an infant. The child could sleep snugly in his cradle close to his parent's bed at night and be moved around in order to stay close to people all day who could rock him with one hand or foot when he wasn't being held. The cradle provides beneficial movement and stimulation as discussed earlier and needs to be standard equipment in any home with infants.

Parents often skip daily baths because, after all, except for the diaper area, how dirty can babies get just lying around all day! But a bath provides an excellent opportunity for touching and stroking and loving a baby. Before my older son, Jaye, started attending school, he often helped bathe his younger brother, Philip. After Jaye enrolled in kindergarten, he would arrive home and demand to know what "we" had been doing all day. He never seemed quite satisfied with my answers no matter how detailed they were. Soon he reverted to bedwetting. I thought it must be the strain of school and of being supplanted by another baby. Not so.

I finally caught on, so I made a few changes. Then when Jaye arrived home and asked what "we" had been doing, I replied, "Nothing at all, we have been waiting for you." I did all the tasks such as housework, washing, mixing formula and so forth in the morning. After Jaye had lunch, we bathed the baby and put him down for his nap. Jaye especially liked smoothing baby powder all over his little brother's body. He was meeting some of his own touching needs but hadn't known how to tell me what he needed. Within five days after my rearrangement of bath time, Jaye stopped wetting the bed.

Another way to handle the bath is by involving Daddy. Either Daddy or Mommy can get in a warm tub of water and hold the baby so he is sitting on the abdomen and resting against the raised thighs. After the baby has been washed, rinsed, and played with, the other parent takes over and dries and powders or puts lotion on and dresses the baby in nightclothes. Then the parent in the tub is left in privacy. Of course, parents should alternate as far as who stays in the tub and who puts the baby to bed. With both parents involved, the baby gets family togetherness and lots of touching this way. Care should be taken that this bathing procedure becomes a pleasurable ritual and not just another duty to be performed.

In India, Mothers regularly massage everyone in the family and then teach their daughters the techniques. It has been remarked upon how relaxed and good natured Indian children seem to be. Perhaps our children would be relaxed and good natured also, if we were to touch regularly.

After the baby is bathed or while diapering, you could apply powder (cornstarch is good) or lotion as a lubricant for a baby massage. Classes are even being taught now in how to massage your baby. You can do it this way: gently stroke the baby's arms, legs, back, chest, and tummy, making sure every square inch of skin is covered. Make this your most soothing touch. Then lightly but firmly pat the baby all over, unless it is bedtime and he has difficulty going to sleep. This is good for you, too, as it stimulates the tactile areas in your own brain. Anytime the baby needs soothing or quieting for sleep, you can repeat this massage. It works wonders for any age.

Anytime a baby who is well fed, comfortably dry, and in no pain cries, he could be telling you in the only language he knows that he needs intimate physical contact. So touch your baby when he cries. Babies do not simply like to cry. They just don't have the verbal ability to express their most powerful needs. We aren't accustomed to thinking of babies as having tension or soreness in their bodies but they do, particularly in the first year. When we do unaccustomed activities, we ache and so do babies. And we know how good a massage feels to us even though at the time we may become even more aware of our discomfort and pain is in our body.

Experiment with different types of touching to see which your baby prefers. He may prefer different types at different times depending on whether he needs stimulation, quieting, or loving. So try all of these until you know exactly when and how your baby wants touching.

As you begin to experiment with touching your baby, proceed carefully! A child has tender, sensitive skin and can only handle a fraction of the pressure an adult or even an older child could. Too light a touch is preferable to too much firmness.

SCRATCHING: Very gently with only the tips of your fingernails brushing the skin (make sure the nails and cuticles are smooth) cover the entire back area.

STROKING: Using the fingertips, lightly stroke the front, back, and sides of each limb. Then do the back and front.

MASSAGING: Using a little firmer pressure with the palms of your hands and fingers, cover the entire body in circular motions.

PATTING: Carefully and gently pat (not slap) all over the baby's body using the entire hand. If the baby is very small or your hands are very large, just use your fingers to pat. Don't tap with just one or two fingers but pat with all of them together.

TICKLING: Occasionally you may find a baby who enjoys being tickled. This differs from scratching in that the tips of the fingers are used in faster circular movements for a longer period of time on each area. The tickling should be *very mild*.

SKIN TO SKIN: Remove any clothing covering your chest area and all the baby's clothing—okay, a diaper could stay—and hold the baby against your bare chest. If it is cool, cover the both of you with a blanket. Many babies never experience this type of skin-to-skin touching.

CRADLING: Experiment with holding the baby tightly, and another time loosely, cradled against your body. For the tight cradling, use both arms to securely and firmly enfold the little body. For loose cradling, use one arm to firmly but lightly hold and support the baby. Some children dislike any type of tight holding or restraint; others need it.

ROCKING: Try this in two different ways. First, sit in a straight chair and gently sway with the baby from side to side. Move from the waist or from the hips. Then try it moving backward and forward (you can use a rocking chair for this).

JIGGLING OR JOUNCING: Holding the baby upright with head slightly above your shoulder and one hand on his back and the other beneath his bottom, move the baby up and down. You may find you move your own body up and down, also. Find a rhythm.

LEBOYER TECHNIQUE: Let your hands slowly traverse the baby's back, one following the other like ocean waves. One hand begins a stroke as the other ends, maintaining a steady rhythm. Do this ever so *slowly*.

Doubtless, after the discussion of some types of tactile stimulation and the need for touch in infants, you can imaginatively create your own touching rituals. Please do. A good book to read to tell you exactly how to massage a baby, with accompanying pictures is *Infant Massage* by Vimala Schneider. Remember, as the baby grows, the *ways* of touching may change, but the *need* doesn't.

5 ○ The Need for Touch Continues

Gradually, during adolescence, the major need to touch and be touched, suppressed and depressed for many years, becomes not only an impersonal search for sensory fulfillment but also a symbolic search for love—for intimacy, security, acceptance, comfort, and reassurance.

Memories become a part of us. Not just images, skills or behaviors, but memories of needs and of satisfaction of those needs. Our cells record and can relive moments of touch.

What mother's body cannot remember the kick of a baby within her womb? What mother does not recall the feel of an infant in her arms or against her breast and does not feel an almost physical ache when she sees a particularly appealing baby? Not an ache to *have*, merely a desire to hold it close. Is there any unfortunate person who does not have memory of lips against lips in a special kiss, or skin against skin in a warm embrace? When we are hurting, sad, depressed, we feel a need to be held because our skin, our body remembers how it felt and how it helped. We associate love with touch, and because our cells hold these memories, we *want*. What we do with this want depends on our age, our particular subculture, family, friends, and our own recognition of our needs and desires.

What happens as children grow and develop? Does the need for touch cease? Does the biological need become translated into other needs, or is it satisfied in other ways? The evidence says no. The problem is that our American culture is anti-touch and, as history remarkably documents, anytime anything is wanted but suppressed, some other way is sought for satisfaction.

Desmond Morris, writing in *Intimate Behavior*, says that as children grow, they willingly turn away from touching and intimate contact as a means of asserting their independence, of preventing envelopment by the mother. He characterizes three stages of changing intimate needs as the baby becomes the child and then the adolescent: "Hold me tight," "put me down," and "leave me alone." He then connects this sequence of changing intimacies to a repeating pattern. In the first stage, young lovers say "hold me tight" and even call each other "baby." Stage two becomes "put me down" as one or both of the married couple find their independence threatened. Then they enter the "leave me alone" stage just as they did in adolescence. But this time they divorce.

When I first read Morris' analysis of these stages, I said, "Yes, that is what happens." However, for a number of reasons, I now reject his analysis. One, he believes that "the need for security, which extensive body contact with the parent has satisfied so well meets a growing competitor, namely the need for independent action. . . ." The child does have a need for independent action, a need to separate himself from the parent, but I also believe that the need to be held and touched remains. I do *not* believe that the "need for extensive body contact with the parent has been satisfied so well." A child merely wants touching and holding on his *own* terms and on his own time line.

Another reason I disagree with Morris' theory is that as a child grows, he increasingly learns *not* to touch. He learns that he may not touch certain things, animals, body parts, and persons. The curtailment and prohibition of his tactile experiences are firmly imprinted on his mind. These prohibitions become "no-no's"—taboos, social anathema and dangerous. If he ignores and violates these restrictions, he will be at least reminded, perhaps chastised or punished. He will feel guilty and think that touching must be either wrong or dangerous. In other cases, the child may be so deprived of touch that he becomes ill. Most of us grow up inhibited, suppressing our most basic mode of communication in favor of what few rituals, ceremonies, and symbols of touch our society deems acceptable. Perhaps because of this, touch becomes a potent behavioral force.

In our culture, the "weaning" from touching behavior between child and parent begins around five or six. Freud saw this as the height of the so-called Oedipus Complex in which the male child harbors sexual desire toward his mother. The Electra Complex, also courtesy of Freud, refers to the same situation between the female child and her father. Usually the two are combined under Oedipus Complex. My, how one man's ideas that sex underlies all human motivation and behavior have permeated our society! We begin to see healthy, caring, loving behavior as sexually oriented or perverted.

At this age, five or six, the male child both begins to evade and to be denied tactile stimulation and comfort through touch. "You're a big boy now," "You're too old to be rocked and held," "Don't cry, be a man," he is told. The father begins to draw away and encourages the mother to do the same. After all, he's not a baby anymore. The boy child observes that little girls are often hugged but, after all, he isn't a "little girl."

Girls enjoy the comfort and reassurance of touching for a longer period, but this usually ceases altogether with the beginnings of breast development or the onset of menstruation, at least as far as the father is concerned. This constitutes another reason I disagree with the theory that children willingly turn away from touching and intimate contact. As I explained this theory to my I.P.C. class one day, a girl, seventeen years old, burst into tears. "My father hasn't even let *me* hug him since I was twelve. He just pushed me away one day. We used to be so close and now he won't have anything to do with me. I thought he hated my body," she said. Later she explained to me that understanding why he pushed her away helped some, but that it still hurt. "After all, he is my father," she said. Eventually, she talked to her father about the situation. Yes, he had heard of Freud's theories and yes, he was uncomfortable when she started developing. They talked, they hugged, and one young girl felt loved again by her daddy. Regrettably, not all situations of a similar nature turn out so happily.

During the period of approximately five to twelve years of age, a child's interest in his body does not lessen even though tactile stimulation from his parents may drop off. What child has not played "doctor" or peeked at parents' or siblings' bodies when unclothed. However, societal restraints and parental admonitions, whether overt or subtle, have asserted themselves and the child begins to feel he is doing something wrong and feels guilty. Besides, at this time his world begins to expand, and other activities and people occupy his time and attention. And so, a so-called latency period occurs with respect to tactile stimulation for girls and, especially boys. I say *so-called* latency period because I think most of the nontouching behavior at this age is culturally induced, not self-induced.

A young man wrote me of a family he is living with while attending college:

> . . . *and they have this sweet nine-year-old girl whom I just love to death. But she does have some problems (hyperactivity and a slight mental retardation) and she just wants to be around me all the time. She is always wanting to tickle me, kiss me, climb over me, or something like that. Now, of course, I enjoy attention like any other human, but when you can't even find time to read a book or to practically even think, it can be disheartening.*

If he only understood this little girl's deep need for affection and touching, then he could *attentively* touch her. He could satisfy her need, then find time to read and think and neither of them would be "disheartened." When we don't understand the needs of others or of ourselves, we often lose patience.

When I first began learning about touching and the need for it in children, I despaired. I thought it was too late for me. My sons were 11 and 16. For a long time it did seem to be too late with Jaye, my oldest son. He resisted my attempts to hug him. Not so with my younger son, Philip. I explained as simply as possible that I was learning about touch, and I had a need to be hugged by both boys. Philip immediately obliged and then asked me to scratch his back. He still loves having his back scratched, and I still get my hugs. With Jaye, it took another four years before he felt comfortable with touching and being touched.

At the time of puberty, tactile sensitivity and experiences become stronger and more frequent. At first, touching communication reasserts itself, as basic human nature will not be denied. Observe young girls strolling with their arms around each other's shoulders or waists. Girls begin to spend the night together, to have bunking parties, giggling, touching, and lying close. Patsy, a twelve-year-old, invites favored friends for "stay outs" and asks them to hold her while she puts her head on their shoulders. Fatherless and with a mother who has little time or interest in her, she fulfills her need for touch as best she can. Boys become increasingly interested in sports and the body contact that they offer. Denied touching contact with parents, at least to any great extent, and learning that it is not socially acceptable to touch in other ways, they attempt to meet their needs through sports and other means.

A visit to any junior high school amply demonstrates how youngsters meet their needs. Girls huddle close together and touch each other's arms, shoulders, hair, and clothing. They hold books close to their bodies and constantly touch themselves in grooming and preening gestures. Boys jostle each other and scuffle in mock fighting. They pull girls' hair, they wrestle each other—all in the name of adolescent behavior. Girls may still receive some touching from their mothers, but because boys seldom do, they often engage dad in roughhousing.

A mother of four advises another mother having difficulty with a fourteen-year-old via the column of Ann Landers. She counsels, "Let her know you love her . . .

touch her a lot. This is important! When she's glued to TV and you pass by her chair, reach out and pat her. Give her lots of hugs and don't be put off by her groans or pulling away."

As children grow up, masculine and feminine roles become more clearly defined by what portions of the body must be covered, where each sex can be acceptably touched in public and how and by whom. A code becomes established for touching. Lines of demarcation are set up and woe to those who violate them! Each person begins to give off subtle but unmistakable cues on his touchability. The adolescent learns about sex and how scary and secret and dangerous it is. Each young person gradually learns to respect unwritten rules on approaching, touching, stroking, taking, or otherwise invading the sanctity of another's body and personal possessions as defined by our culture.

Gradually, during adolescence, the major need to touch and be touched, suppressed and depressed for many years, becomes not only an impersonal search for sensory fulfillment but also a symbolic search for love, for intimacy, security, acceptance, comfort, and reassurance. With the important avenues of touching fulfillment through parental contact and friends usually blocked off, the adolescent learns to seek fulfillment through sexual exploration. He experiences with himself and others, and if he fails in these areas, he learns to avoid any contact at all with others. Some adolescents simply draw into the shell that is their body.

Society has added one more item to the "don't touch" shelf of taboos. Besides fear of pleasure and Freudian generated fears, now we have added the fear of homosexuality to further curtail touching behavior.

Into the area of the tumultuous teenage years comes

much confusion about love and sex, touch, and caring. The first time I said to my group of seniors in I.P.C. that I believed that much of what went on in the back seats of cars, or motels or wherever, was not so much a need for sex as a need to be held, to be touched, to be affirmed in a most fundamental way, to reach outside their own bodies to find gentleness, tenderness, and understanding, I expected either embarrassed silence or denials, at least from the boys. I got neither. They agreed. They already knew. Now you must understand that we had a very special trusting atmosphere in that class, and we had agreed to either always tell the truth or to stay silent until we could. The boys talked and the girls talked. The boys said that sex still remained a big factor and sometimes it was hard to control their urges, but the touching, the holding was the real thing. It was what lasted. They said they were afraid—afraid that if they didn't at least try to put the moves on the girl, to have sex, to go all the way, girls might think them unmanly. And every class said essentially the same things, with only a few exceptions from those whom the kids called the "macho men."

We used to hug a great deal in my classes and do simple touching exercises like head tapping or shoulder rubbing. At first much giggling and discomfort attended the exercises, but not for long. The disturbing thing was that the students still had to be careful about touching outside of class. In their words, "The rest of the world just doesn't understand yet." I always told them, "You are a part of the rest of the world. Change it! At least change your part. Do it by talking about this different way of viewing touch and by touching your friends, your parents, and eventually your children."

So after adolescence, what? As we become adults,

many opportunities for touch are lost to us. There is less overall contact with parents, including the physical contact, and fewer friends to interact with. We use more words to communicate. However, the kind and amount of contact in adulthood varies from person to person. It depends on the age, sex, situation, and relationships of the persons involved. Certainly couples experience some touching if only in sexual intercourse, and parents of young children have opportunities to touch.

Our society has turned increasingly to the paid or licensed toucher. There may be other reasons rather than touch to seek paid services, but certainly body contact, a definite by-product, may serve to increase the frequency of usage. A client with several small children reported with surprise what a co-worker had said to her, Which was: "I haven't been touched for weeks, and I had to go to the doctor to get that." We have massage therapists and the dubious massage parlors, hairdressers and barbers, chiropractors, medical doctors and on the touching fringes, encounter and body work groups and counselors.

If you doubt the satisfying nature of physical contact from a licensed toucher, you have only to closely observe men in a barber shop. I waited at a barber shop for a man so I could take him to an appointment. Although late, he sat in the barber chair after his hair was cut so he could enjoy the scalp and neck and shoulder massage. I watched the barber apply a soft whisk brush around his face and neck, and the brushing of the man's shoulders in case any hair had gotten under the covering cape. Asked later why he'd looked so pained and why he didn't just leave after his haircut, he said, "But I love going to the barber shop—it's a high point in my life. I wish I could go every day." This came from a man who was not only a nontoucher but ordinarily disliked being touched by anyone else, especially men. But it was okay for the barber to touch him; he had a license!

I'll speak about other aspects of such types of touching in other chapters, but before I leave the subject, I want to discuss older adults. As we age, opportunities for touch grow even less. If one-half of a married couple dies before the other, as is very common, touching for the survivor may disappear almost entirely.

A newspaper account of a hospice for terminally ill patients tells the poignant story of a widow with cancer. A minister came to the hospice once a week to visit the patients and would hold the lady on his lap and gently rock her with her head against his chest. At first, she was a little frightened of this strange and unaccustomed behavior. Then she began to look forward to his visits. The sense of security, comfort, and love sustained her in her grief, pain, and sense of hopelessness. She began to improve—remission, they called it. Then the minister was transferred. The new one visited only occasionally and offered only a few moments of words and brief, embarrassed eye contact. The woman now waits to die, and in truth, the doctors say that for some unknown reason her condition has recently declined sharply.

Sally, a friend of mine, tells of her dying grandmother who had never been very affectionate, suddenly wanting to hold all the babies she saw and to be kissed and hugged whenever anyone came or went. She spent her days rocking and fingering objects.

Is it, as some say, that we regress as we grow older, or is it that our touching needs have always been present and now are not even minimally satisfied? Perhaps, our touching needs become stronger, more urgent, or we think as we age that we have "permission" to touch without being misunderstood. Maybe as we become older we find the wisdom and courage to attempt to satisfy our needs.

Another friend recounts the story told of a younger friend's father-in-law after he became a widower. At age 80, he kept trying to get into bed with the young woman. "Just to talk," he'd tell her. "I can't do anything." The young woman said she knew he needed some comforting touching, but she just couldn't. She cared for him, she said, but she just couldn't do it. I cried when I heard this. I cried for the old man's need, I cried for the young woman's inhibitions and I cried because I wasn't sure what I would have done if this had been me a number of years ago. If she could have just held him in her arms in a warm hug it would have helped them both.

Whatever the age, all of us need touching, especially when we are scared, depressed, lonely, or tired. Nothing else can express so much, offer so much solace and safety, so much tenderness and soothing as loving touching.

Does the need for touch continue at a constant level throughout our lifetime? Does the need wax and wane at different ages? There is, as yet, no definitive answer as to the need for touch at different ages; and indeed, there may prove to be as many answers as there are individuals. However, for now there *is* you and me. Together we can explore the available information and ask questions and seek answers within ourselves and within the people with whom we come in contact.

6 ○ Restraints on Touching

We aren't giving our children enough loving touching for them to distinguish between loving and sexual touch.

 Touching as a means of communication is learned early in childhood, and unless subsequent learning intervenes, it persists throughout life. So, touching is culturally learned behavior. Many cultures are highly touch oriented; others are not. Highly touch-avoidant cultures include Germans, English, English-Canadians, and white Anglo-Saxons. Italian, Russian, French, South American, Mediterranean and other cultures are highly tactile. America's culture, notwithstanding the many ethnic groups here, is also touch avoidant. There are numerous reasons for this. Aspects such as age, sex, religion, race, marital status, economics, manhood myths, power and status, fears, and deprivation influence our touching behavior.

Anthropologist Ashley Montague states that Christian teachings in the past (and most denominations now) fostered a tradition of fear of bodily pleasure. Since touching brings pleasure as well as comfort, it became a sin.

Taboos grew up around tactile pleasures, and guilt and fear either made touch a forbidden fruit or prevented it altogether. Other research on the influence of religious training or background on touch behavior substantiates this and shows a definite pattern.

Christian religions, particularly fundamentalist Protestant religions, discourage touching. Several studies have found American Jews to be more highly touch oriented in space orientation and gestures. Non-Protestants touch more regardless of age or sex. Changing societal norms have begun to influence behavior to some degree since younger Protestants touch more than older Protestants. It is a shame that out of ignorance and fear so many puritanistic religious groups deny and suppress a need that is so essential to human well-being.

A few years ago, I received a letter from a young minister in training, 22 years old, who had never had a serious relationship with a female. Mickey had never kissed a girl or even held a girl's hand. He worried about it quite a bit. He had just started dating and didn't know how to handle things. How could he? He'd never been touched lovingly, in his memory, or seen others lovingly touch. He equated touching with sex, and his religious beliefs said no sex until marriage; so, he had been deprived.

Economics may also play a part in our society's prohibitions against touching. We place such a high value on private property that the "don't touch" admonition is applied to things and then transferred to people. We learn not to touch other people's property, not to bother Mother's books or Daddy's tools, not to touch toys that belong to other children. No wonder that children become hesitant to touch at all. In addition, they've previously been warned many times about touching certain people and body parts. So they confine their touching explorations to safe things or to situations where they won't be watched by adults. They become secretive about their touching.

Another aspect of economics that influences our touching behavior is the philosophy of scarcity. From this comes the concept that if things are the measure of man, and if there aren't enough things to go around, then we must be concerned about acquiring them. This preoccupation with the acquisition of money and the things it can buy makes us view work as a duty and pleasure as sinful and immoral. We become stiff, life-rejecting creatures who feel more comfortable touching objects that we own than we could possibly feel touching each other.

As our world becomes more crowded, we become more zealous in guarding our own personal space, that invisible boundary surrounding our body into which we do not allow intruders. We become like porcupines. We need to get close enough for some warmth and companionship but must stay far enough away to avoid pricking one another. This personal space isn't spherical: that is, it doesn't extend equally in all directions. It has been compared to a snail shell, a soap bubble, it's been called an aura, or referred to as breathing room. It differs with cultures and is portable territory that we carry wherever we go.

Invasions of our personal space are common in hospitals, during police interrogations, and in crowded elevators, among other places. Personal space is not only culturally acquired but essentially a daylight phenomenon. For example, we dim the lights for intimate occasions. Lovers, when pressed together to kiss, close their eyes. Dimness or darkness eliminates distractions, of course, but mostly it permits closeness. Since we learn our individual differences during our early years, people deprived of touching often have a problem with personal space in that they will approach too close or stay too far away.

We can observe our own personal space by approaching people and observing their reactions. I had just made this observation to a speech class and emphasized that most people had an average frontal boundary of 18 inches and that people would back away if at all possible if you intruded into their space. At that moment, there came a knock at the door. I told the class, "observe this," and invited the messenger, a girl, to come in. I approached to about 18 inches, and she thrust a note at me and began backing out the door.

Of course, the class thought that was great, a real demonstration of the principle of personal space in action. We continued discussing and there was another knock. "Oh, try it again," they cried. So I did. This time the messenger was Jim, one of my advanced debaters. I approached and approached and came still closer until I was embarrassed. There we stood almost nose to nose, and then Jim (of Italian descent by the way), reached out and hugged me. After he left, I had to explain a little more to my group! Familiarity, trust and affection decrease the personal space required for protection.

Try the following exercise to explore personal space, both yours and others. First, get a yardstick, and thoroughly familiarize yourself with how far in front and to the side of you 12 inches, 18 inches, and 24 inches is. Try walking up to walls or people, and then measure the distance until you feel confident with your internal yardstick. Next, without telling them what you are doing, approach standing people. Approach from the side first and then try it frontally. Try this with:

- Friends of the same sex,
- Friends of the opposite sex,
- Strangers,
- Intimates—spouse, lover, parents, children, and
- People you work with.

When approaching you can stop as soon as you feel that the other person is uncomfortable. Estimate the distance and you can get a fairly accurate picture of your own personal space. If you want to explore others' space, continue until they either move away, put up something as a buffer between you, look strained, or say something like "what are you doing?" I would add a word of caution, though, about invading others' personal space. Some people become downright belligerent about it!

Experts have also contributed to our touching inhibitions. I mentioned Dr. Holt in an earlier chapter. J. B. Watson, a widely followed early behavioral psychologist, gave some similar advice in a 1928 book called *Psychological Care of Infant and Child*. He advocated treating children as young adults, and at the most, kissing them good night on the forehead, although he preferred just a kind word or smile. He urged leaving the child alone in a well-protected yard for the better part of the day. He firmly advised against coddling as well as cuddling, and told mothers never to kiss their children, nor to pick them up and rock them, and not to caress them. To do so would produce children, so said Watson, who were totally incapable of coping with the world they must later live in. It is difficult to believe that he was serious. But serious he was, and many parents tried to emulate his teachings. Have you heard any parents echo his sentiments? I have heard many do so.

Another reason for the prohibitive and punitive attitude toward touching that continues virtually unchecked today is the association of touching with sexual intercourse. True, intercourse does require some touching, but *not* the type of touch we have discussed. Many aspects of this confusion between touching and sex exist.

Let's look first at the confusion between two very similar words. The first is *"sensual,"* meaning gratification of the senses. However, it is further defined as indulgence of appetite, deficient in moral and spiritual affairs, carnal, gross, and finally, sexual. There is a time and place for sensual touching, and we'll discuss it later in a chapter on sex.

For now, look carefully at the next word: *"sensuous,"* which also means a gratification of the senses, and pleasure. (Note the period.) That's it—no sexual implication or connotation at all. But people really get these two words confused. I'm concerned with *sensuous* touching. If you really want to remember the difference, look at it this way. The sexual kind of gratification ends in *you all* (little play on words there) as in *sens u al*. The simply pleasurable kind of gratification ends in *you and us*, as in *sens u ous*. What we need more of in this world is *sensuousness*.

Another problem concerning touching and the association with sex has to do with what I call the **PHOBIA SYNDROME.** The following conditions or situations all point to an abnormality in our thinking, in a lack of loving touching, in a confusion about love and sex, and to a self-fulfilling prophecy that touching is dangerous and turns people on sexually, particularly men, and that they then have no control over their actions. This syndrome concerns our societies fears, labels and judgements.

"P" is for Promiscuity, a term often applied to any person who has many casual and touching friends even if the relationships are not sexual. Ironically, it also seems that some people who are promiscuous engage in casual sex because they need the touching so desperately and know no other way to get it. It is easier for someone to offer himself sexually and have the offer accepted than it is to ask for a back massage and be refused.

Next is "H" for Homosexuality. Outside the realm of sexual activity, females are allowed to engage in more touching behavior with other females than with males. Males, however, avoid same-sex touching. With the increasing prominence of the Gay Movement, other segments of society increasingly prohibit and condemn same-sex touching, especially between males. There seems to be much fear and condemnation attached to homosexuality. But keep in mind that it isn't catching! You either are or you aren't gay, and you won't become homosexual by touching members of the opposite sex.

The "O" stands for the Oedipus Complex (lustful desires on the part of the child toward the opposite-sex parent). Freud so frightened the wits out of us that

mothers of teenage sons often shy away from affectionate contact with them for fear of arousing lustful desires.
However, our children, in order to learn to differentiate
between hands that touch to turn on and hands that touch
to convey comfort and affection, must experience both.
Infrequent touch heightens its impact and clearly sends
the message that touch is dangerous and very private,
which in turn, puts it into the world of sex. For the adolescent this is dangerous territory without a guide and certainly must be kept very private.

We've already discussed how a father often stops hugging his daughter at a time when she needs it most because he's afraid to embrace her now that she has breasts.
True, adolescents often seem to reject, at least outwardly,
affectionate touching by acting shy and grown-up. Parents
fall into the trap.

"B" is for Body Areas which can present a problem
as to where to touch. Generally speaking, only the hands,
arms, shoulders, and head are seen as non-sexual areas.
We can place a hand on the shoulder of a friend or ac-
quaintance but not on the chest or behind or the leg, lest
we run the risk of misinterpretation. Of course, the type
of touching also carries a message but, by and large, in our
society, we confine our touching to the safe areas, meaning those body parts seen as non-sexual. The problem is
most evident in regard to opposite sex touching. Sometimes any touch to any body part is misconstrued as sexual in nature.

"I" is for Incest. Incest is perhaps not so much an
increasing problem in our society as a more publicized
one. Incest, as with other sexual crimes, is a tragedy for
those involved, especially the innocent victims. However,
the solution is *not* to tell our children, "Don't touch or let

anyone touch you." We have done that and it hasn't worked. What this method has done is to promote even more confusion and restraints on touching. The situation is indeed complex; yet there must be some place to start besides limiting touch with our siblings and parents.

And finally "A" is for Adultery: this is what so many people believe happens if you have opposite sex friends after marriage! But, it is not necessarily true. I have many opposite-sex friends as do other women I know. I touch these male friends, but I wouldn't dream of going to bed with them for a myriad of reasons. Those who assume that there is a sexual relationship between opposite-sex friends are the ones who have the problem. Fear in the form of jealousy and possessiveness runs rampant in our society. This seems to relate to the attitude of scarcity discussed earlier in the chapter.

Marriage is still an important cultural part of our society despite the widespread prevalence of divorce. At least 80 percent of divorced people remarry. Formerly, the bonding effect of touching within marriage, combined with moral restraints, precluded opposite-sex touching outside of the primary relationship. Today, however, there seems less assurance that the two partners will restrict their touching behavior. Many people actually feel freer to touch after marriage. For one thing, rejection can be coped with more easily. After all, if the other party does reject you, he or she is not necessarily rejecting you but your marital status, so you can rationalize. Also, the marital state is demonstrable proof of a person's basic heterosexuality; thus, members of the same sex may touch more. In addition, touching may be less inhibited for the person who believes that being married removes desire or sexual connotation from touching.

The PHOBIA SYNDROME is a problem for many reasons. It indicates that we don't give our children enough loving touching for them to distinguish between loving and sexual touch—not enough touching for them to identify the touch that is psychologically uncomfortable, not healing, not soothing, not friendly, not consoling, and not loving. It indicates that in our true sexual relationships we don't enjoy enough satisfying body intimacy and, thus, pair-bonding. If our primary relationship satisfied our touching needs, we wouldn't need to worry about secondary relationships with others.

The PHOBIA SYNDROME simply indicates the extent to which our society inhibits touching by equating touching and body contact with sexual interest. The touch element in relationships is overstressed in primarily nonsexual relationships. This is not to say that there may not be minor sexual feelings or confused feelings, due to our upbringing, in our nonsexual relationships but they do not have to be acted upon.

Two cultural bits of fiction that men, for the most part, accept are that (1) affection isn't for men, and (2) affection equals sex. As you can readily see, if these statements were true then men would have no sex since sex is not for men! But excuse my facetiousness. These two stereotypical myths prove a real burden for many men.

Myth 1 results from bringing up boys so that they feel it is somehow, sissy, unmanly and weak to express feelings or show affection, which, of course, includes touching. Little girls can be "huggy and kissy" but not little boys.

Myth 2 means that even though at times men might just want attention and touching, they either refrain or turn the need into a sexual thing. How many times have you heard a man say, "I don't want to start something I can't finish," and all he's talking about is a hug or some cuddling!

Status and power also play their part in deterring touch. A wealthy person would be more likely to have license to touch a poor man than vice-versa, as would a doctor with a patient, a teacher with a student, an employer with an employee, an older person with a younger person, and a male with a female. N.M. Henley in *Body Politics: Power, Sex and Nonverbal Communication* argues that the male predominantly initiates touch; and that this is as likely to be an indication of power as an expression of affection. Whereas, if women initiate touching with men, it is more apt to be associated with sexual intent since any implication of power on the part of a woman would be unacceptable. I distinctly remember one occasion when I experienced male touch as an indication of power. I was teaching at the time, and a new principal had made some drastic changes in my classes and schedule without telling me. I discovered it on the first day of school. Angry, I confronted him. He stood up and patted me on the head and tousled my hair. I knew immediately his attitude toward power, and I certainly didn't like it.

Henley's research also suggests that certain situations could have an inhibiting effect on touching behavior. People, in what I term, "one-down" positions, will be more inhibited in situations such as:

- Asking for advice or information,
- Responding to an order,
- Agreeing to do a favor for someone,
- Being persuaded about something,
- Being at work rather than a social affair,

- Being on the receiving end of someone's excitement,
- Talking with someone on a casual level, and
- Telling someone about one' worries.

Observe yourself and others in the situations listed above and notice how touching inhibitions are present.

Definite restraints also exist concerning touching and older people, not in *their* touching of others, but in their *being* touched. Older people are more likely to be avoided, although as I said earlier, they do have a greater license to touch, at least in this country. Others tend to touch them only in a functional or professional way. Institutionalized or hospitalized patients, such as residents in homes for the aged, are seldom touched. Social structure and sex taboos in our culture, especially in nursing or caretaking situations, seem to hurt those in the greatest need of help. Certain factors determine the touching behavior. An older person is more likely to be touched if he is the same sex as the caretaker, if touch is not required close to the genital area (the further away, the more touching), if the touch initiator has a higher social status, and if the patient has a relative absence of physical impairment apparent in his appearance. Since females usually comprise nursing and caretaking personnel, it often follows that in institutional settings the male, the severely impaired, and the patients who look bad are most likely to go untouched.

Margaret, a resident of a home for the elderly, told me I was the only person to hold her since her husband died. Her daughters and son gave her a perfunctory hug of greeting sometimes, but nothing more. Face it, our culture does not give us encouragement to touch objects or people who are not aesthetically pleasing to the eye. Most of us find the very thought of touching a snake distasteful. Yet for those of us who have stroked the skin of a snake or at least timidly patted one, it is not an unpleasant experience. Snakes do not feel cold, clammy, or slimy. Neither is the skin of an older person unpleasant to touch. We have only been subtly taught so.

A man of forty, prematurely wrinkled by years of work and exposure to the sun, told with pain filled eyes of his young son looking at his father's hands as they reached out to pick him up and saying, "Ugh, you're old. I don't want your wrinkly old hands on me." The father hurt. I cried. It was my husband and my son.

Another restraint on touching behavior occurs when we refuse to take responsibility for our own actions. Some people try to justify their refusal to initiate touching (although they are often open to receiving) by saying that they just aren't good at it. "Sorry," they say as they excuse themselves, "I just never learned." And some, even sadder, just don't care.

Certainly our fears inhibit our touching behavior, too. We fear being rebuffed or rejected; we fear being misunderstood, and we fear the sexual association. We also fear intimacy because we've been so deprived as children. We all struggle with our need for love, and the two biggest obstacles are deprivation of emotional love and touching and a fear of intimacy. If you haven't had enough of the first, then you will end up with the second—a fear of intimacy. Fear of intimacy is more common than you might think. So many feel the need to be separate, to be self-sufficient as a protection against being disappointed in life. Getting too close to someone might cause dependency. Getting too close to someone might cause us to see ourselves reflected in the other, and we might not like what we see. We seldom recognize our fear of intimacy, rather we rationalize our emotions and behavior and point the finger of blame elsewhere. Our apprehension about intimacy says to others: meet my needs, take care of my barriers, but don't get too close while you're doing it.

Listen with your inner ear to this internal dialogue, a comment on our fear of intimacy:

> *How marvelous to be intimate,*
> *No qualms at all with closeness.*
> *You as companion, together in love,*
> *I'll share my innermost self.*
>
> *I'll tell you all my secrets.*
> *But you might leave, yes, you might.*
> *Then I'd be alone once again*
> *And hope denied would surely hurt.*
>
> *No qualms at all with closeness.*
> *Oh, promise me you'll stay!*
> *But promises aren't commitments*
> *And even commitments aren't certain.*
> *Is there nothing that will last?*
> *Is everyone here today, gone tomorrow?*
> *No, don't come close, don't touch,*
> *I've decided it's too risky after all.*

We've talked about many of the factors that influence our touch-avoidant culture. We've examined some societal restraints. But what we must remember is this: you and I *are* society. You and I make up our culture. Many authorities hold little hope for any changes in our tactile behavior until we change our child-rearing methods. I feel more optimistic. I believe changes can be made at any point in our broad spectrum of society and be effective. No one can take the initiative for us. We can't rely on others or on society to bring us the fulfillment we need or desire. Many years ago, my students were constantly saying, "But *they* won't let us," or "*They* wouldn't approve." The "*they*" that they referred to were those people out there, society, our culture. Well, *WE* are *they.* And if we want to bring loving, caring, soothing, healing, comforting touch into our lives, then we must do it for ourselves. If we want to end the confusion between a loving touch and a sexual touch, then we must do it ourselves.

The chart on the following page could help eliminate some confusion between types of touches. Consider first the interpersonal level between people, then the emotional level and then the type of touching appropriate for each level. You might use the chart to check out your interpersonal interactions or those you observe around you. I did this recently. At a social affair I encountered a man I used to know and whom I felt friendly toward. He put his arm around my waist, and I realized I heard a little warning bell in my head. When he said good-bye and kissed me full on the mouth, the bells really went off. I hadn't realized we were in a caring interaction. You might construct your own personal chart differently according to your cultural background. The key word is *appropriate,* so if you are open to touching, not inhibited by fears or societal restraints, then construct your own appropriate chart. You may find that it changes over time. Mine certainly has.

APPROPRIATE TOUCHING IN INTERPERSONAL INTERACTIONS

INTERPERSONAL INTERACTION	EMOTION	APPROPRIATE TYPE OF TOUCHING
Superficial	Little/none	Accidental/handshake
Ritual, inclusion, small talk	Acceptance	Handshakes, back pats, arm, elbow, shoulder
(Each succeeding level includes the preceding levels)		
Sharing ideas, opinions, judgements	Friendly, sympathetic	Quick, brief hugs, head pats, squeezes of hand, arm around shoulder
Caring, emotions, needs, hopes, fears	Affectionate, empathic	Full-body hugs, arm around waist, kiss on cheek or on mouth briefly, rocking, holding hands, tender face cupping
Loving, trusting, openness, sharing of heart and mind	Tender	Sensuous: foot, hand, body massaging, holding closely and lengthily
Romantic, desirous, sharing of heart, mind, and body	Passionate	Sensual: mouth-to-mouth kissing of long duration, body stroking and contouring
Erotic, total intimate sharing of heart, mind, and body	Sexual	Caressing and stimulation of all the erogenous areas of the body

About eighteen years ago, I had my "awakening" to the need for touch. Although, I was not raised in a touching family, I made a personal decision about how I wanted to be regardless of the misunderstanding or rebuffs I might receive. The first person I reached out to happened to be a student. Sherry came to me after school one day, sobbing hysterically, and ended up huddled miserably in a corner. I put my arms around her, but she struck out at me after a few moments. However, those few moments seemed to forge a special bond. Afterwards, I became acquainted with her family and came to understand her touch avoidance. She was definitely deprived. A few years ago, I visited her to see her new baby, and we embraced. As I watched her with her baby, I was glad that years before I'd had the courage to reach out and continue touching despite the initial rejection.

After my father died, I knew that my mother would need another source of touching and affection. In my family, we didn't even say, "I love you." But I said it to my mother on the phone one day. A long silence ensued and then in a small voice, she said good-bye. I persisted for about three months. Then one day at the end of the conversation, she said, "I love you, too, Phyllis Kay." I went around with a smile on my face all day. It had felt good to say the words and it felt wonderful to hear them back. In addition, I started hugging her when I arrived for a visit and as I left. At first, it was like embracing a stiff piece of cardboard and continued like that for a long, long time. But at least she got to the place where she didn't push me away. I won't say I didn't feel rejected at times or doubtful about my persistence. I did keep reminding myself that I had chosen how I wanted to be regardless of misunderstandings or rebuffs. Finally, one spring she attended a stress class (touching helps reduce stress, too) in which we were doing touching activities. She immediately called me to her side and said she'd just watch, since she wasn't a member of the class she wouldn't participate in the exercise. But Mother ended up getting a facial massage and giving one. She felt uncomfortable at first, but she did it. And liked it!

A few months later, I went back to my old hometown and there on a table in my mother's living room was a newspaper article written about me and touching. I'd given it to her at least a year before and she'd never said she had even read it. Later in the day, as we stood watching a parade, my mother slipped her arm around my waist and there we stood. I was flabbergasted. I whispered to my sister, "What's going on here?" Her reply was, "She's been this way since she came back from visiting you. She even hugs me!" Not too many months after that incident, Mother attended a group I held at my home on learning to love yourself. Before she left that night, she had hugged everyone there! I was elated. She needed the touching, and so did the others. One more barrier down.

I could talk more about my husband, sons, friends, students who have learned to touch and be touched. But I think you have the idea now. I'm no different than you. I'm still not completely free or comfortable in my touching. I'm learning as I go along. The restraints are there only because we allow them to be. The barriers are within each of us, not out there. So, explore yourself. Learn all you can about touching. Open your heart—reach out to give a loving touch.

7 ○ Effects of Deprivation of Touch

We go to great lengths to satisfy our skin hunger without ever realizing what it is.

 Before you read this chapter, please do the following activity first. It works best with another person. If you absolutely must do it alone, then do the activity with someone else at the first opportunity.

1. Ask the other to roll up his sleeve, take off his shirt or whatever is appropriate for the situation. You need as much bare arm as possible, preferably from shoulder to fingertips. Also, ask that all jewelry be removed.

2. Sit facing the other so you can comfortably reach the bare arm.

3. Have the other close his eyes and sit quietly and comfortably.

4. Gently begin to stroke, pat and rub every square inch of skin between shoulder and fingertips.

5. You should remain quiet while touching.

6. Continue this touching for at *least* two full minutes.

7. At times you need to lift and turn the arm. Be gentle and respectful.

8. Finish with gentle but quick and firm patting all over the arm. Return the arm to its original position and say this:

   Keep your eyes closed, and sense first your touched arm and then the untouched arm. Note any differences between the two. When finished, open your eyes and tell me about any sensations and differences between the two arms. Thank you.

9. After listening to the other person, reverse the process and complete steps 1 to 8 with *your* arm being touched this time.

The usual sensations reported in the touched arm as opposed to the untouched arm are lightness, pleasant heaviness, tingling, relaxation, warmth, feelings of aliveness or energy. Occasionally, you will encounter someone who feels no difference between the two arms. In this case, try doing it for a longer time and make your touch a little more stimulating. Consider the untouched arm as being deprived and keep the differences in sensation firmly in mind as you continue to read about deprivation of touch. You now have a point of references for descriptions of feelings and effects.

From our discussion of the need for touch in infancy, we can clearly see that deprivation of touch in the first year of life can be fatal. Infants without adequate loving touching just waste away with marasmus. If a child in its first six years does not receive adequate tender loving care and touching, then we can predict a number of things about him as an adult:

1. Some degree of physical and mental retardation will be evident.

2. A weakness in the physiological system may manifest itself in childhood or later in life as psychosomatic illnesses.

3. He will have an inability to give or receive affection. This could manifest as a person being unable to comprehend the concept of love or being unable to feel any emotion deeply. Such a deprived person might turn out to be a "loner" or drift from person to person (or marriage to marriage) always searching outside for what he lacks within. Unable to successfully relate to others, rejection would commonly occur, and he could well end up not only alone but feeling sour about what he assumes life has dealt him.

4. Deprived of physical and emotional closeness, he might develop an extraordinary need for affection in later life that would be next to impossible to fulfill. He would feel alienated, deprived, and frustrated. He would feel he had so much to give and no one to give it to.

5. He would be resistant to being touched or touching and be termed **"touch avoidant."**

Children from homes with loving, touching parents look and act differently than those who are rarely touched. Touched children feel better about themselves and are less hostile, more outgoing. Well-touched children almost seem to glow. Sidney Simon says you can tell the children who are getting their touching needs met by their clear eyes and an effortless flow of energy throughout their body.

What is adequate touching? How many strokes, cuddles, pats, or rocking movements a day translate to adequate? In truth, we do not know. Possibly it varies from person to person or maybe there is some standard that applies to all of us. However, most researchers, anthropologists, and psychologists agree that, given the touching restraints and behaviors in our culture and the studies done with animals and comparisons with human beings, few, if any of us in this country, receive adequate tactile stimulation and loving touch.

We can speculate on the connection between child abuse and deprivation of touching in childhood with some amount of certainty. We have long known the connection between a child who has suffered abuse becoming, in turn, a child abuser. When the pleasure centers in the brain are deprived of touch and movement stimulus, the person will have difficulty experiencing pleasure and develop an unquenchable need for it. Unfulfilled, the need often manifests itself as cyclic violence.

Child abusers usually have a low frustration tolerance, a feeling of being deprived of pleasure and thus unable to give pleasure to another. They have feelings of alienation and isolation and a quick temper. The abusive parent's pattern of behavior is reminiscent of the experiments in the 1950s and 1960s dealing with social isolation and monkeys which showed that deprivation of mothering resulted in monkeys whose behavior varied from hyperactive to apathetic to violent. Isolated monkeys who became mothers often had to be restrained from abusing their infants.

These deprived monkeys turned out to be socially inept and often held and rocked themselves as do autistic children. Later research, using Harlow's isolation-reared monkeys, concludes that the influence of the environment seems to be imprinted on the brain structure and, in turn, shapes the environment. In other words, brain centers concerned with touch, movement, and emotions such as affection are either damaged or incompletely developed due to lack of touching and rocking.

The importance of touch in adulthood can be inferred from James Prescott's studies of body-contact practices. Specifically, in one study of 49 primitive cultures, Prescott found a correlation between low levels of infant affection and high levels of violence. Primitive societies that prohibit or punish early touching behaviors and premarital sexual affection also exhibit such social trends as slavery, wife purchasing, fears of castration, theft, exhibitionistic dancing, sexual disabilities, and the killing of enemies. Apparently the restriction of outlets for physical pleasure and skin stimulation results in frustration and efforts to seek other forms of stimulation, most of which are counterproductive to a society.

As a low-contact culture, our country has exhibited, at times past and present, all these forms of counter productive forms of stimulation and frustrations. Look at the signs of it. The violence in our society has reached epic proportions, and we have a low level of infant affection. We think we have eliminated slavery until we consider the relationship between pimp and prostitute. We no longer engage in the practice of buying wives unless we consider the practice of rich men (or women) using inducements of wealth to attract marital or sexual partners. Psychologists tell us that although fears of castration are no longer as prevalent, sexual disabilities are on the upswing. One need only go out on a Saturday night and observe people on any dance floor to recognize our exhibitionistic tendencies. Then comes the killing of enemies. Well, since the turn of the century, how many millions of men, women, and children "enemies" have we killed in the name of protecting our values, wealth and country?

As far as premarital sex is concerned, the "sexual revolution" of the 60s and 70s has tapered off. The polltakers tell us that the number of young people engaging in premarital sex has dropped, although it may not seem that way because of the increased openness about the subject. Many believe, as I do, that the sexual revolution had little to do with sex and a lot to do with a need for love and touching. During that period of time, a great many people, mostly the young, protested against war and violence and human indifference. They wanted to change things. They especially wanted love.

Prescott found something else in his studies, something important for us regardless of our age. He discovered that those societies with loving and touching child-rearing practices, but which prohibited premarital sexual affection, were nonviolent. Societies that maintained more rigid and harsh child-rearing practices, but were liberal in allowing premarital sexual affection were also nonviolent. Does this mean that even if we were deprived as children, even if we've deprived our own children, that hope remains? This study seems to indicate it is never too late. In other words, intimate, pleasurable contact in adolescence can counteract the deficit from childhood. This is of paramount importance to us in our culture. Perhaps, we may even find that intimate, pleasurable contact in adulthood can also counteract the child-hood deficit.

Behavioral scientists have given this deprivation of touch the term *skin hunger*. Which is defined as hunger of the skin, the skin needs; hunger as in starved, famished, an appetite for, a desire for, wanting. The term meant little to me when I first read it. Then, one day as I led a group through some touching exercises without participating myself in them, I felt it. I first noticed it on my fore-arms, then my chest area, then my whole body, like an aching. Remember when you hear an old song that brings back bittersweet memories, or you recapture a poignant moment, something painfully or sweetly piercing that affects your feelings? It is like that. A yearning that is *in* the skin. A want. A wanting to be touched, to be held, a deep-seated hunger for physical contact through touching and being touched. It affected me profoundly. So, I thought, this is what skin hunger means. It was the first and last time I ever allowed myself to fully experience the sensation of skin hunger. The intensity frightened me. But, I think it necessary that everyone experience this skin hunger completely once in their lives. If you do, then you, too, will understand without my words, the need for touch.

Some people confuse skin hunger with restlessness, loneliness, or stomach hunger. We go to great lengths to satisfy our skin hunger without ever realizing what it is that we need. We attempt to satisfy it with food, with drugs, with entertainment, by burying ourselves in work, in talk, in activities, and with promiscuity. Yet it remains, this desire for the most basic form of communication—touching.

We are all born with skin hunger and we manage to satisfy it only to some degree. It is not confined to the young; it is with all of us. In *Caring, Feeling, Touching*, Sidney Simon says:

> "Clearly, there are hundreds of thousands of adults prowling around our pornographic society who were not touched by their parents, and who do not touch their own children, who will not touch their children and so, dreadfully, on. Adult victims of skin hunger pass on to children their own confusion and conflict about love and sex, touch and caring, and the crucial differences between hands which touch to heal and comfort and hands which touch only to 'turn someone on.'"

If you needed someone to touch you now, to hold you, to affirm you without words, with a soothing, comforting, loving touch, to whom would you turn? I sincerely hope you could turn to someone or perhaps many who would willingly satisfy that need. It seems to me it would be worse to have someone in my life whom I asked for touch and was refused than to have no one to ask. Either way the touch need would go unsatisfied, but if refused, then you bear the added burden of rejection.

In our society, we have relegated touch to five symbolic areas. **The first area is that of rituals.** Rituals include handshakes, dancing, a pat on the back or perhaps even an embrace in greeting or good-bye—so long as it is in appropriate locations such as airport terminals, train depots, or bus stations. More intimacy and longer touching are observed in good-byes than in greetings. Perhaps, we feel safer that way since, as the other person is leaving, it constitutes no threat. Or maybe the emotions have just built to an outpouring level.

Barbara, a divorced friend who travels a great deal,

told me her son gave big wonderful bear hugs. Then she said wistfully, "But he doesn't always meet me at the airport."

"Won't he hug you when you meet at home?" I asked.

"Oh, sure," she replied. "If I asked him, he'd be glad to. But it seems, well, you know, different at home."

So Barbara often does without the hugs she wants and needs if she doesn't have the airport to use as a socially appropriate place.

The handshake, especially between men, is a time-honored tradition in our social structure. Women have also begun to shake hands more often in business situations. Since the handshake's purpose is to affirm another's identity as an equal-status person operating by essentially the same rules of conduct, women in business need this type of touch. The pat on the back or handshake of congratulation is also part of our cultural ritual, as is a perfunctory kiss of greeting or a good-bye in some circles and circumstances.

The second symbolic area is that of hostility. Fighting, disciplining, and contact sports are a fertile area of body contact. Some young children need touching so badly they will deliberately provoke parents or teachers. In schools today, physical disciplining is practically nonexistent. But with parents, the behavior will often escalate until the parent jerks, slaps, or spanks the child. Of course, the child also gets attention along with the touch that he craves. One form of educational therapy called "Transactional Analysis" refers to an overwhelming desire for "strokes" which are any acts that imply the recognition of our presence. When the need for positive strokes remains unmet, the child looks for "negative stroking," which can almost always be procured. Often children in a family will resort to fighting or roughhousing to get the touch they need. In addition to the roughhousing my boys did at home, my oldest son, Jaye, the one I raised with less touch, once told me that he loved high school football and would really miss all that hitting, pushing, and tackling. "You know, Mom," he said, "all that body-contact stuff."

I have to laugh at men who minimize the need for touch, especially "macho" types, when I watch contact sports. There's a whole lot of touching going on there. The players huddle with arms around each other; they slap hands and have lots of other contact inherent in most sports. Consider the football coach ready to send in his quarterback to save the game. While telling him what to do, the coach's hand rests on the quarterback's shoulder or his arm or around his back. When the moment comes for the quarterback to take the field, the coach gives him a pat of confidence on his rear and often nearby players follow suit. Also, consider what the team does after an important point is scored or after they've won the game. Everyone hugs and pats and holds on to each other. No wonder contact sports are so popular with men!

Also, contact sports provide a popular means for **vicarious touching, the third symbolic area in which we allow touch.** We can sit in the stands or in front of our TV and indirectly participate in all that contact. Furthermore, we can watch TV shows or movies showing touching and lovemaking and experience it secondhand, too. Regrettably, there are some people so touch deprived that they can't stand watching someone else touch. Not only do they not touch, but it even upsets them to watch others touch. I know a teacher who gets violently angry when he sees high school students daring to hold hands in the hall. And if they hug—well!

Professional touching is the fourth area. The intent of touching here is to perform some service, to accomplish some task. In order to prevent any possible intimate or sexual messages from interfering, the person to be touched is usually treated as a nonperson or object. This objectivity becomes necessary in order to allow the type of touching. This might be a gynecological, genital or prostate exam, a tailoring measurement, a session with a golf or tennis pro. Barbers, chiropractors, hairdressers, physicians, massage therapists, athletic trainers, and foot reflexologists all fall into the professional touch category. Some people are never touched except vicariously or by professionals. Some people make unnecessary trips to doctors just to be touched, although they often do so on an unconscious level. In a conversation reported to me recently, a woman said to her friend, "Well, I saw my doctor today. He touched me, and it's the first time I've been touched in months."

I would suggest that if your touching needs must be satisfied by professionals, that massage therapy (not massage parlors) and foot reflexology provide the most honest, direct, and gratifying methods. Some chiropractors would run a close second. Not only can touch needs be satisfied to some extent, this type of touching is extremely healthful. Please note that the farther we move from strictly task-oriented professional touching behavior, the less socially sanctioned the profession becomes. Thus, the professional areas that best meet touch needs are less socially sanctioned.

Grooming constitutes the fifth area. We've already discussed licensed groomers such as hairdressers and barbers, but a lot of touching is performed under the guise of grooming. People brush or stroke or push wayward hairs back into place. We straighten each others collars and hems, tuck in blouses and skirts, pick cat hairs off clothing, remove price tags for people. We check out the texture of fabric when someone else is wearing it. We clean up spills on people. We apply lotion to unreachable skin, put pockets back in, tie bows or ties, work on pimples and blackheads, remove chiggers. Chiggers? A man I know equates this grooming with loving. One of the ways his mother showed she loved him was by removing chiggers while they were still fresh. Yes, you can see chiggers! Armed with a magnifying glass (although his mother did it with sunlight and her naked eye) and tweezers or a needle or pin, you can actually locate the little red devils and lift them off. He swears by this! His mother, although discouraging other physical contact, did "groom" him, so that now this is one of the ways he solicits or allows physical contact with a loved one. So grooming can be a way of satisfying the need for touch.

There are medical consequences for adults who do not have their touch needs met. A University of Maryland researcher has noted for both sexes and for all races in the United States that unmarried people have high death rates, sometimes as much as five times higher than those of married individuals. In *Broken Hearts: The Medical Consequences of Loneliness*, Dr. James Lynch says that the death rate from heart disease among unmarried adult Americans runs two to five times higher than for marrieds. That's a big difference. The death rates for single, widowed, and divorced persons area also greater than for married persons from a combination of cause—car accidents, cancer of the respiratory system, cancer of the digestive organs, stroke, suicide, cirrhosis of the liver, rheumatic fever, hypertension, pneumonia, diabetes, homicide, and tuberculosis.

Is loneliness the only cause, or does the scarcity of

touching have a lot to do with it? We know it does with babies, with children, and with older people, so it does not take too great a leap of logic to suppose it also does with unmarried persons.

Dr. Lynch showed how important human contact is. He observed the fluttering heartbeats of heart attack victims in intensive care wards and noticed that the heartbeat calmed while the nurse took the patient's pulse, and returned to an abnormal beat after the nurse released the hand and left.

Of great concern in regard to the deprivation of touch is the number of children caught in divorce. This number has tripled even in the face of declining birth rates. Parents can reduce *contact* with their children for a short time with no apparent difficulties, but over the long run, serious emotional and physical problems may appear that may shorten the child's life three or four decades later.

Touch deprivation can affect us psychologically or emotionally. While doing a guided imagery to recall some events during teenage and childhood years, a woman named Geri suddenly reported to me being in what she first called nothingness. She saw very bright light, white all around her, and felt what she could only describe later as a sense of nontouch. She felt little emotionally. Neither of us knew what to make of this. Of course, we speculated endlessly. Then, about six months later, she accidentally discovered she had been born prematurely and placed in an incubator for several months. Since this occurred in a small Kansas town in 1950, we can assume that an isolated, bright, warm environment with nutrients and medications was provided. Touching needs were probably not attended to at all, as they weren't recognized as important than—nor are they often now.

Today, through much exploration and understanding,

Geri has gone from being touch avoidant to welcoming touch. She is highly sensitive to being touched and can't imagine getting enough touch. She thinks it would be impossible to meet her touching needs though she is trying with a bi-monthly massage. She also has numerous physical problems and had to deal with a feeling of being invisible, as if people don't really see or recognize her as a person, which is understandable considering the way her life began. The wonder is that Geri does not exhibit more psychological damage.

Doctors in the field of orthopedics have experimented with touch techniques and have published extensive and detailed records of children who show stunted mental and physical growth when deprived of their mother's touch. One such touch deprived three-year-old's bone growth was found to be just half that of a normal child's.

As indicated in chapter 2, we know that many skin problems have emotional causes. Virtually every emotion involves interaction with this outer covering. I have found that physical touching and what I sometimes call "inner touching" or emotional therapy often solves the problems. If we do not cry, express anger, remember traumatic events, or call for help, our skin does it for us.

John Naisbitt, in *Megatrends* says that as our society becomes more technological, a counterbalancing human response of touch must occur or the technology will be rejected. He says, "The more high technology around us, the more the need for human touch." He believes that the human potential movement with its accompanying discipline and concept of personal responsibility is a critical part of the *high-tech/high-touch* balance between our physical and our spiritual realities.

Perhaps, the fad beginning in 1983 with Cabbage

Patch dolls has helped fill a psychological and physical need in even the biggest children. As we attempt to come to grips with our loneliness and touching deprivation, some of us try to fill this void by touching or hugging an object. Maybe cuddling up to a Cabbage Patch doll helps fill this need, especially since they are so "ugly" that they produce the instant emotional reaction of wanting to give the poor misshapen waifs the love they must surely need.

By examining the effects of the deprivation of touch, we find that there are four primary values of touching.

The first is the biological value. Numerous studies have indicated the importance of touching and physical stimulation of infants. Physical, psychological, and even social development seem related to early touching experiences. Without touch, infants do not learn to signal their desires in order to receive the care they need, and so, they will develop physical problems. Recent hospital studies have shown the impact of human touch on people in comas and on heart patients.

Second is the communication value. Touching is the tangible form of communication between parent and child. Touching continues to be an important channel through which the child signals his needs. Many messages and emotions can best and sometimes *only* be communicated by a touch. Studies in hospitals with terminally ill patients reveal that touch is the "language for good-bye." Thus, we begin and end our lives with touching as the mode of communication.

The third value is psychological. We learn through touch. Physical contact has great bearing on the child's sense of security and well-being. It is an established fact that emotionally disturbed children respond well to physical stroking and holding. Severely mentally disturbed adults often sit hugging and patting themselves. Gentle physical contact seems to provide a universal source of reassurance and comfort when we are emotionally distressed. Touch is required in order to establish a self-identity and an adequately pleasing body image. It is also necessary to the development of satisfactory self-esteem.

Social experience is the fourth value and recent research seems to be developing into a pattern linking the quality of our touching experiences to our competence in interpersonal relationships. The ability to trust others and the ability to be sensitive to the needs of others directly relates to touching. Many marital problems have been traced back to inappropriate childhood touching experiences. In addition, research has shown that cultures which give a lot of physical affection to infants have a low incidence of theft, murder, and rape.

If at this point you are feeling your own skin hunger as a result of touch deprivation or feeling guilty because you've deprived your children or others of needed touch, then stop a moment and reconsider. To add sadness, yearning, resentment, anger, guilt, or any other such emotion to the weight of the original deprivation is useless. You don't deserve such a heavy burden. You, I, and our parents have done the best we could within the parameters of our knowledge and past social restraints. That is in the past. This is now. And right now you can decide how you want to be and how to meet your needs and the needs of others today, tomorrow, and in all the tomorrows to come. You cannot change the world; you can change yourself.

8 ○ Lovemaking— the Sexual Touch

Men persist in thinking of touch as only a sexual trigger.

 So far, I've discussed only the loving touch —nonsexual touching. Let us turn our attention now to lovemaking, touch in sexual situations. First, we will look at some general information. Due to our cultural upbringing, females are, for the most part, more sensitive to touch than males at all ages. Erotic arousal for the female depends more on touching, whereas the male depends more on visual stimuli. In romantic novels this phenomenon might be verbalized this way:

> *He undressed her in his mind. Beneath the modest dress, he imagined her rosy nipples and the soft fur covering her mons. As he drew her to him, she melted at his touch. As his hands caressed the softness of her skin, she felt heat sweep through her body, and her lips opened to him.*

In real life situations, just as in romantic novels, it is the male who primarily initiates sexual touch The traditional feminine role encourages touch as a part of warmth, comfort and general expressiveness. In most *other* types of relationships females initiate more touching. It seems that females learn to accept even a slight touch and to respond to it more favorably than males. Yet, in sexual relationships, females have often learned to minimize their touching so as not to arouse the male too soon. On the other hand, females need to touch and to be touched for full responsiveness and, therefore, depend on males to do so. Remembering that major tactile areas in the brain are stimulated by touch with hands, fingers, and lips, we see that males benefit greatly by giving touch.

Of interest here is the sequence of 12 steps delineated in 1971 by Desmond Morris in *Intimate Behavior*. These steps define the courtship patterns of animals (including humans). Variations may include diminishment of the sequence, different ordering of the steps, or embellishments. In times past, the progression from step to step took considerable time. Perhaps you remember, that as a teenager there were certain "do's" and "don't's" on the first date, second date, and so on. Now the sequence seems to be speeded up. A single friend, Stephanie, said she found out quickly how things worked following her divorce. To quote her, "Friday nights are for looking and picking someone up, Saturday night is for 'dating' and Sunday morning you say good-bye and thank God you had someone to be with over the weekend." Consider that as you read through these adapted steps, and you will realize the rapidity required to meet and bed within a few short hours.

The progression from courtship to intimacy looks like this:

1. **Eye to Body:** We look at another person and subconsciously determine the attractiveness quotient for us. If they score highly enough, we proceed to the next step.

2. **Eye to Eye:** If we know the person, we engage in mutual greeting signals. If we see a stranger, we usually watch him or her surreptitiously. If we find the stranger attractive, then we manage to glance at the same time and perhaps smile. If a positive response is given, we proceed.

3. **Voice to Voice:** We note the signals exchanged by tone of voice, accent, content of speech, etc. If the two people continue to be mutually attracted, they move to the next phase.

These first three stages could occur in seconds or over a longer period. The next step could occur quickly as in a greeting handshake, or it could be delayed considerably.

4. **Hand to Hand:** This step involves the first actual touching and is often performed under the guise of "helping" behavior—lighting a cigarette, assisting across the street, putting on a coat, and so on. Prolonged hand holding will wait until the relationship has been openly declared.

5. **Arm to Shoulder:** The usual method is for the man to put his arm around the female's shoulders. Since friends also embrace this way, it is unlikely to meet with rejection.

6. **Arm to Waist:** This advance definitely moves in the direction of romantic intimacy.

7. **Mouth to Mouth:** The kiss combined with a full frontal embrace is a major step because it creates a strong chance of physical arousal in both, especially if the kiss is prolonged.

Formerly, the steps 8 through 12 required days, weeks or months to complete—if ever completed.

8. **Hand to Head:** The lover's hands begin to caress, stroke, and hold each other's face, neck, hair, and all about the head.

9. **Hand to Body:** Now hands begin to explore the partner's body, squeezing, stroking, fondling. The male usually begins to manipulate the female's breasts. As physical arousal begins to reach a high level, the female may call a temporary halt if she wishes to stop before completion of the sex act.

10. **Mouth to Breast:** Now requiring privacy, the interaction becomes the prelude to not just arousal, but arousal to climax.

11. **Hands to Genitals:** Caressing of the partner's genitals soon begins to stimulate the actions of intercourse. Gentle, rhythmic rubbing and stroking, with the male perhaps inserting his fingers into the vagina. This stage could lead to orgasm.

12. **Genitals to Genitals:** Here, the couple reaches full copulation.

Major variations of this sequence occur in rape and loveless mating and with people who engage in sexual athletics. In other words, making love is not the aim, but merely physical satisfaction or psychological dominance. In such cases, the later genital stages are not considered as part of a sequence but as ends in themselves.

The purpose and value of the 12 steps are many. Just by completing all of the steps, lovers can relieve themselves of the intense frustration of "petting" or the fixation on masturbatory activities. The two dangers still existing are pregnancy and venereal disease. However, the primary value of the steps when they are spread out over some time is that each stage will serve to strengthen the attachment of the couple to each other so that they will want to stay together after satisfying the sex drive.

Without this step-by-step bonding and continued strengthening of attachment and affection, one of the partners, usually the male, or both will move on to seek another partner. Women by and large, have less interest in casual sex than men do, even though sometimes they think they should have more interest or wish they did. Women require an emotional involvement of some sort from sexual activity. This doesn't mean a woman can't be seized by physical passion or won't search out many sexual partners. It does mean that any attraction won't be purely physical and that being promiscuous proves difficult for most. Also, many studies have shown that a woman is less likely to experience orgasm with one-night stands than in a long-term relationship.

In *Sex and the Brain*, Durden-Smith and Desimone state that woman has an evolutionary program that has helped her develop mechanisms of protection.

"For if sex is to be had, she has to say yes, she has to be convinced that there is no danger in their intimacy, that he is gentle and reliable."

Courtship provides the avenue to check out the male's safety factor, the evidence of his intent. She needs to make sure the man will care for her and any children. As a result, women are more careful and show more discretion in their sex drive than men due to a biological programming.

A friend of mine, Nadine, had been single for a number of years following her divorce and in her words, "The lack of closeness and touching and sex is driving me up the wall." She began to embark on a series of one-night stands, although she wouldn't admit that that's what they were. She'd pick up a man in a bar, almost always someone she'd met or at least seen there before, and take him home with her. She couldn't understand why, almost without exception, none of them ever asked her for a date. She struggled with her loss of self-esteem and her loneliness. Then friends introduced her to an interesting man who invited her out to dinner. She knew of his past history with women, and it frightened her. I told her of the courtship steps and their value and she decided not to go to bed with this new man right away. A happy family was the eventual result. Yes, she married him.

One primary reason that men tend to rush into sex is purely psychological. Women want to let a friendship evolve first, but men often cannot allow that possibility. The longer he must wait, the longer he worries about the possibility of rejection. This could also explain the predilection of some men to turn women into sex objects. It is easier to be rejected by an object—or someone inferior—than by another human being of equal status.

From a male point of view, although the availability of sex has increased, something else has remained essentially the same. Men are still expected to do most of the initiating and to risk rejection at each stage of further intimacy. After rejecting a man at one stage by telling him to wait, the woman rarely goes ahead and takes the next step herself. Men can end up feeling very vulnerable and fearful, so they set up a defense mechanism by seeing the woman as an object. Men and women need to work together on their relationships to counter such problems.

To skip courtship stages is one thing. To advance to the later genital stages, not as a part of the sequence, but as an end in itself, leads to sexual athletics, the tyranny of the orgasm, and many sexual problems. Worse yet, the attachment link is not forged; consequently, emotional intensity is lost, and physical intensity must compensate. The greatest tragedy is the loss of touching. You can usually tell when people have started having intercourse. They stop touching! They perform only ritual or perfunctory touching. Females definitely feel the loss, and many men will admit to the same feeling. I want to repeat. When two people consummate their relationship sexually, the loving touching soon stops . In no way can intercourse meet all or even most of our loving touching needs.

Before we leave the idea of courtship steps, I'd like to further suggest that the physical touching stages should parallel stages of verbal communication. That is, each progression in the area of physical touch ought to be matched by a corresponding progression of talking, of verbal communication exchange. Such an attunement would look like the following chart:

ATTUNEMENT

Touching Stages	Verbal Communication Stages
1. Eye to body	*Nonverbal smiles, winks, etc.,*
2. Eye to eye	*and polite rituals: "Hello,"*
3. Voice to voice	*"How are you," and so forth.*
4. Hand to hand	*Small talk, exchange of information.*
5. Arm to shoulder	*Past history, ideas, opinions.*
6. Arm to waist	*Sharing likes and dislikes.*
7. Mouth to mouth	*Sharing of hopes and*
8. Hand to head	*future dreams.*
9. Hand to body	*Sharing of emotions, fears, developing trust.*
10. Mouth to breast	*Full self-disclosure of who*
11. Hand to genitals	*we are on all levels with*
12. Genitals to genitals	*nothing hidden.*

It seems that we often condense the touching stages and skip the latter stages of verbal communication that could forge strong emotional links of love between two people. How much happier and fulfilled we could be with our touching needs both met and attuned to our verbal communication needs. That would truly be called making love.

In the book, *Beyond the Male Myth* by Pietropinto and Simenauer, it is stated that 98 percent of the male respondents were concerned that their partners were satisfied sexually. However, *The Hite Report* by Shere Hite, did not find this at all. Obviously, our society has a problem if the males say they are concerned with the female's satisfaction, but the females don't believe it. Could it be the particular males who responded? Out of curiosity I talked to a man who claimed to be concerned about his wife's satisfaction. I believe I detected a slight blush, then he told me this joke: "How many orgasms does it take to satisfy a woman?" Answer: " Who cares?" He immediately followed with: "Well, that's a male chauvinist joke. Maybe only men think it's funny."

Perhaps it is the case that while almost any man will give lip service to the idea of being concerned with the woman's satisfaction, their behavior may be miles apart from what they say. Men, by and large, assume that they know all there is to know about sex. Translated, that could mean: "If I know everything and am doing it 'right,' then 'who cares' if the woman enjoys the act fully."

Men may not know everything about computers, raising children, or their job and they'll admit that they don't. But when it comes to sex that's another story. After all, with all the time they have spent thinking about sex, reading or viewing pornographic materials, talking to other guys and pursuing sexual opportunities, they ought to know—right? To admit that they didn't would also be to admit that they might not be satisfying their partners. This, in turn, could lead to the thought that they weren't virile "he-men," as society demands. This train of thought also leads to the inescapable idea that since every other man knows all about sex, he should, too.

Have women not told men how to act with them? The authorities on sexual behavior advise women to tell men what they really want, what turns them on and turns them off. This is fine advice *if* the man is open to it. Unfortunately, all too often they aren't. And all too often the woman is uncomfortable communicating this way to her partner, often because she fears injuring his male ego. The communication needs to be honest, straightforward, from both parties, *and* at an appropriate time.

Tom is a man who says the woman's satisfaction is more important than his own. He always makes a point of asking just as he and his partner are in the midst of passion, "Is there anything you want me to do to you?" I wonder what his reaction would be if the woman should at this point prop herself up on her elbow and said, "Well, there are a number of things you could do differently." There is a more appropriate time for this kind of communication. Anyway, regardless of his seemingly open attitude, this particular man is unable or unwilling to discuss sexual matters, beyond the fact that he's "horny", outside the bedroom. Furthermore, he admits he is really only interested in the woman having an orgasm—which to him is the whole point—before he does so, then he can feel okay about having his. Examples such as this one show why male and female surveys differ so much.

Actually, when you talk to men and women about sexual pleasure, it is as though you're talking about apples and oranges. To a man, orgasm is the whole point, the reason for sex, the means to satisfaction. For the woman, touching, emotional closeness and a sense of security are the important things.

In January of 1985, Ann Landers published the results of this question, suggested by a reader, that she had posed in her column:

> "Would you be content to be held close and treated tenderly and forget about the 'act'? Answer yes or no and please add one sentence: I am over (or under) 40 years of age."

Of the more than 90,000 women who replied, 64,800, or 72 percent said yes and of this number 40 percent were under 40 years old. Ann replied in her column, "The greatest revelation to me at least, is what the poll says about men as lovers. Clearly there is trouble in paradise." Indeed there is. Of the women voting no, most said they need the sexual climax in order to relieve physical tension. Many "no's" also said they would feel exploited and used without orgasm.

It would seem, then, that the majority of men are totally ignorant of the workings of a woman's mind, heart, and body. Psychiatrist Marc Holender supports the concept that some women crave being held far more than they crave the sexual act and may even trade off sex for cuddling and the feeling of security it gives. Body contact, he says, "commonly provides feelings of being loved, protected, and comforted. The need or wish for it is affected by depression, anxiety, and anger." Certainly a period of heightened sexual activity frequently occurs at a time of intense emotional need.

Just skin touching skin can be reassuring. Touching and being with another person may be what women crave more than the relief of sexual tension. Being held offers security, protection, comfort, and love to many women. Too many relationships are like two railroad tracks running side by side but never touching. I know of one husband who had taken a massage workshop with his wife. Hooray! thought his wife, believing that now she could get her touch needs met. She gave him long, loving massages and did her best to use all the techniques she had learned. Unfortunately, every massage he gave her ended either halfway through in sexual intercourse—because she feared saying no and he didn't respond to her request to wait—or ended with the husband feeling inadequate because she told him how she liked to be touched during the massage. He now does massages for friends, and she spends quite a bit of money on weekly massages. But at least they are speaking again, and both are getting some of their touching needs met—even if not simultaneously.

I believe that in addition to the problem of ego involvement and the tendency to associate touching with sex, a lot of men just don't know *how* to touch. They don't understand the techniques of touching and caring for a woman. Men often take the direct approach because they fear failure if they go slower. They don't have confidence in their ability to accurately read women's feelings, and they think that if they make a mistake, they've failed. So, they just plunge in as they did when they were 16, 18, or 20 years old. It is also amazing how most men are so ignorant of a woman's body. One man who knew almost nothing explained how to please a woman: "You rub a woman here and then there and it works." Another allows for a kiss or two then goes straight for the genitals.

Women often tell of men grabbing their bodies in intimate places and expecting the woman to like it. Paula tells of how she stopped this:

> "Often I would be in the kitchen working when my husband came home, and he'd come up behind me and grab my breasts. At other times, he'd just reach out and pinch the nipples. I told him it made me feel dehumanized, that I definitely didn't like it. He kept doing it so I began to reach out at unsuspected times or in retaliation and grab his crotch. He stopped the grabbing but he didn't touch me at all for a long time. I had tried to talk to him first, and he just didn't listen. I didn't know what else to do, and then I felt so guilty about hurting his feelings. What I wouldn't give for a little tenderness and cuddling."

Intercourse is so temporary, and orgasmic satisfaction, when isolated from loving touching, lasts so little time. Actually, little contact occurs in the sexual act between many couples. But in reality, all of our body and mind is a sexual organ—not just the genitals and breasts. Lovemaking requires much communication. Touching expresses many emotions, the act of intercourse just one. Intercourse focuses too much emphasis on the male erection, which can and does cause problems for men. On the other hand, intercourse doesn't require as much intimacy as touching; therefore, touching isn't taken as lightly as intercourse. It carries too much impact. Men can fake love by substituting sexual desire and technique, and a woman can fake orgasm without the man really catching on, but you can't fake touching someone lovingly.

Patricia, a good friend of mine, wrote me about concerns she had about touching within her marriage.

"It was John's 'touch' that bothered me. His touch was impersonal—wanting sex impersonally. I didn't realize it then or why I shrank from his touch, but that was it. He had great technique, but there was no love, tenderness, affection, or any reaching out in his touch. He was always an observer, never involved, and his touch told me that, only I didn't know how to read it."

Men do most of the touching in the sexual act, and I have no quarrel with this so long as both man and woman agree to it. The key here is agreement. However, I have a problem with the reasons why this usually happens. One reason stems from the culturally conditioned passivity in women. Another very practical reason is that a man gets sexually excited so quickly. He just doesn't seem to need as much stimulation. Men seem to touch for two reasons, say Masters and Johnson, the famous sexual research team. One is tactile and the other cerebral. The first is because of the sensory feedback he gets from his fingertips and hands moving over curves and softness and smoothness of a woman. The other is the excitement of touching private and formerly forbidden parts of a female body and anticipating what will come.

Many men persist in thinking of touch only as a sexual trigger. Often, their philosophy is: "Touch women in the right places and they will get aroused. Touch them some more in the right places, and they have an orgasm." The how-to-do-it sex manuals don't help much. They replace the idea of touch as a sexual trigger with touch as a technique. Instead of men and women being taught how to lovingly touch, they are taught how to *manipulate* each other's bodies. So touching becomes a technique of stimulation for the purpose of sexual gratification, for reaching a climax, not as a way of communicating love, caring, and tenderness.

Some women contribute to the problem because they discourage any form of touching when they don't feel in the mood for sex. They believe or know from experience that if they make any kind of contact, their men will assume it will lead to sex. The irony here is that such women merely encourage their lovers to associate touch with intercourse. This reinforces the problem rather than helping men to accept and recognize the need for nonsexual touching.

Couples need to communicate more, to negotiate their needs. They need to be able to tell each other whether they want cuddling and holding and touching to lead to sex or not. Otherwise women who refrain from touching because of the sexual outcome deprive themselves—and men—of a lot of good feelings and needed touching. This needs to be worked out ahead of time. Of course, another situation may arise. Many women know themselves well enough to realize that after a protracted period of holding, cuddling, and being close sometimes have sexual feelings surface. That needs to be communicated beforehand, also, with the provision that the touching can become sexual only if both agree.

Touching should not be a service but an exchange of private emotions between two people who love and value each other. Touching is a form of communication, *not* a service, *not* a trigger, *not* a technique. Only touching can bridge the separateness between two people, counteract the loneliness of living in our own skin, establish a bond between two minds, two hearts, two bodies.

One woman says that when she and her lover talk about his emotional upsets, and he allows her to touch and comfort him, she feels very close to him. Ironically, she also says this is about the only time she really wants sex with him.

Tender, loving, touching establishes a trust that other words and actions cannot. Touching by stroking the skin, exploring the texture, investigating the contours of bone and muscles can be an end in itself and can convince the person being touched that he or she is loved, valued, and cherished as more than just a sexual partner. Touch can also be an end in itself, as a means of experiencing the tactile pleasure involved in stroking and being stroked.

Are we so deadened that nothing but a full-fledged orgasm truly moves us? When we look at the sensitivity of body parts, the genitals do not take up much sensory cortex in the brain. Remember the diagram of the body representing the sensitivity of various parts?

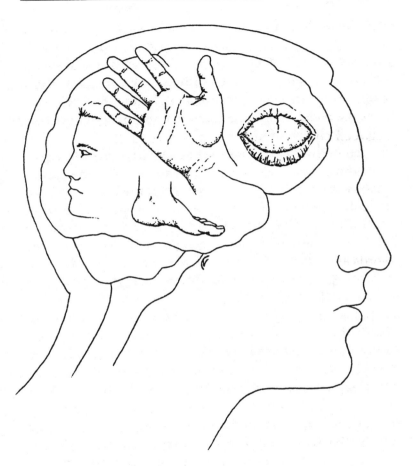

THE MOST SENSITIVE TACTILE AREAS
REPRESENTED IN THE BRAIN

Notice that the genital area is not one of the most sensitive. The *thoughts*, the *emotions* and the massive *tactile stimulation* of the whole body triggers sexual desires and orgasms. Women who have difficulty achieving orgasm may simply need more tactile stimulation—touching—all over the body. This is assuming that the emotions are conducive to lovemaking.

To further explain why there is such a widespread sensitivity to sexual touch despite the fact that the sexual organs are not strongly represented in the brain, we need to look at several factors. When two people first begin to interact with each other, a man responds to visual stimuli, and his sympathetic nervous system immediately becomes activated. This is analogous to the accelerator of a car being pressed down with all systems set to go. The female usually responds to the male signals as if responding to danger, and her sympathetic nervous system also becomes activated. Then, hormones signaled by the brain and sensory systems come into play. Brain circuits controlling pleasure and reward are activated, and they send chemicals to deep brain structures responsible for emotion and motivation.

All of these systems, influenced by hormonal messages, constantly communicate back and forth until both are aroused. The right chemistry causes sparks in the beginning. What he sees and what he thinks turns the male on. The female responds to his excitement and touch as well as the "danger" and emotions involved. Indeed, both men and women can become heavily *addicted* to this stage of activation. The man may actually carry his response further but by seeking a new and different woman each time, thereby becoming a "Don Juan." If the woman desires to go no further and prefers staying at this stage of activation, prefers basking in the sense of power and feeling of being ardently desired, others may consider her a flirt or a tease.

Later in a relationship, a male still can become excited by his thoughts and visual images. He also has the built in aggressive urge for sex. However, the female needs the emotional involvement coupled with touching. Also, the foreplay, if it continues long enough (15 minutes to an hour), consisting of massive tactile stimulation from full body contact, skin against skin, lips against lips, hands stroking and caressing, will take the place of the initial excitement in activating her nervous system. But, after the establishment of a sexual relationship, most couples use touching as only a nonverbal way to indicate a willingness or a demand to have intercourse.

Most men, then, regard touching as little more than a waste of time and effort, or as a technique to use to satisfy the woman. The woman who wants the loving touch, the tenderness, the reassurance of herself as a person, may comply to the man's wishes initially, but at some point *she may begin to regard intercourse as he does touch—a waste of time and effort, something done only if absolutely necessary or if feeling especially benevolent toward the other.* Is it any wonder then that we ask "Where does all the romance go?" or that we feel that sex is something that automatically becomes boring and less satisfying after being with the same partner for a while. Is it any wonder then that women overwhelmingly say they would rather men hold them close and treat them tenderly and forget about the actual sex act?

One man who discovered his wife was having an affair asked why since she got plenty of sex at home. She told him, "But that is *all* I'm getting. No love, no touching, no talking—just plain sex." So the question should be, are you making love or having sex?

In a search for reasons for sexual attitudes in our society, we must look at the possible adverse effect of pornography on our touching and sexual relationships. The worst kinds depict women as an orifice with two globular sexual protrusions, the least offensive or ''soft porn'' depict women as glistening, perfectly shaped seventeen-year-old bodies—as only objects for sexual fulfillment. All cater to the idea of man as aggressor and women as ones who pant for the male penis. Because I fear censorship and favor education and spiritual values, I quarrel not so much with pornography as with the lack of balance in the media catering to and influencing male attitudes. Where are the beautiful pictures of friends touching friends, parents hugging their kids, older people being tenderly cared for? Where are the stories of how touch affects our lives and our emotions? It wouldn't sell?

Men buy most pornography, so perhaps women should buy pictorial touch books for their young children and stories for the older child about loving touch. They should be required reading. The news media could publicize loving touch as an alternative to pornography rather than just reporting the battles ensuing over ''smut.'' We could have not only pets to handle in grade school, but we could teach children how to touch other human beings lovingly. Maybe then as males grow up they would be more tender and more touching and women would not only know what they need but speak up for what they really want.

Studies presented at the annual 1985 meeting of the *Society for the Scientific Study of Sex* depict the American woman as a victim of male sexual attitudes. Among college women surveys found that from 5 to 19 percent, ''an alarming minority,'' do *not* consider forced sex to be rape.

Many men *and* women find it acceptable to submit to unwanted attentions on dates. Reports from across the nation, Washington State University, Texas A&M, Mills College in Oakland and Cornell University in New York, echo the appalling statistics and attitudes. One psychologist stated, "Women are massively victimized in this society at all levels of their relationships, particularly women who are just beginning to date in high school and college."

One study involving 439 female and male students found that 5 percent of women and 19 percent of men do not believe that forcible rape on dates actually constitutes rape nor view the male's behavior as unacceptable. These students found nine circumstances that could justify forcing a date to have sex. None of these had anything to do with what the woman might want. Instead, the reasons represent an attitude among men that men are superior to women. An extension of this attitude is that the primary purpose of women is to please and satisfy male needs. The reasons deemed acceptable by students for forcing a date to have sex were:

- If the man spent a lot of money on the woman,
- If she "led him on,"
- If she had sex with other men,
- If she was intoxicated, or
- If she excited him.

These reasons illustrate attitudes that view women as something to be bought and paid for and as totally responsible for arousing male sexual desires.

The problem here is that men are raised with, or

choose to have, unrealistic expectations about sex that can prove to be a real problem for many men. Sometimes men feel that women enjoy affection and touching but hold back when it comes to sex. Conversely, women may feel that men don't want affection and touching, just sex. Neither is true. Men and women both have affectional, touching and sexual needs. The problems stem from cultural myths and lack of communication and commitment to each other's needs.

Men and women so often worry about the physical infidelity of a partner. Once a women has "given" her body to a man and once a man has "possessed" a woman, they begin to feel jealousy and possessiveness. They want to control what they "occupy." I see another kind of fidelity as more important. If we define being faithful as "a commitment to the pleasure, continued growth, and well-being of the other," then we see what real fidelity means. Let us commit ourselves to this kind of faithfulness and then we needn't worry about someone else "taking away" something from us.

When men want sex frequently or act as though they do, they may not always realize that they really need affection—to be held and touched. Men also need the feelings of acceptance, comfort, reassurance, and approval that can come from being lovingly touched. They know how to ask for sex and have been taught that it is quite acceptable to do so. They don't always know how to ask for nonsexual affection and touching.

Most men, if willing, can learn to truly enjoy holding and caressing and stroking and hugging and lots of tender communication. I believe they yearn, though it may be unconscious in many cases, for this. They would reap many benefits if they would learn to enjoy this kind of intimate communication. Their needs for touch, however submerged, would be met. They would have partners who felt free to express their physical affection without worrying that it had to turn into sex. They would find their partners, if pleasured in ways they want and need, would be willing to pleasure them in ways they wanted. Most of the relationships and marriage problems could be cured if those involved could reach out and touch each other.

When one cuddles and holds and strokes, one is simultaneously parent, child, friend, and lover. As one woman says, "I can have sex with a lot of men, but why bother. Most men don't cuddle, don't really touch except to try to turn on. I don't need that very often, I can masturbate myself and not end up feeling depressed or devalued."

Perhaps it is scary to touch lovingly precisely because it draws you so close to someone that you become more vulnerable, more emotionally dependent, more open to possible rejection. Occasionally, the woman is the one frightened of touching and closeness. Vanessa, after 18 years of marriage, learned to touch, to caress, to be tender with a man because her lover insisted she stay in his arms after intercourse. He considered that the "best time to be together."

"It is ironic," she said, "that I was so resistant when what drew me to him was one time when I heard him say, 'too many people don't know touch can be tender.'" Vanessa said that sometimes when they made love she felt so loved, so tenderly cared for, so totally open and vulnerable, so cherished, so close, that she cried. It took her months before she realized they were tears of joy.

The range of touching needs is especially wide and especially important after intercourse. Some love to cuddle: some find contentment in merely lying close with

hands and legs or some part of their body touching the
other. Others automatically reach for a cigarette or leap
out of bed to wash away the odors and fluids of sex. Men
are more prone to run than women. Women often complain that their partners don't want to snuggle after sex.
Of course, some women also do this. Regardless of who
does the running, the other may feel "empty-hearted,"
possibly angry orfrustrated. It seems the one who leaves
has had enough of intimacy and intensity and the snug-
gler wants more. The need to be held and touched
tenderly after sex has much to do with reassurance that
all went well and that they are still loved—or loved for
themselves.

Physical differences can partially explain why men
copulate and run. Just as a man becomes more quickly
aroused, so does his sexual interest drop off rapidly once
he has achieved orgasm. But lovemaking is much more
than just the achievement of a climax; it is a microcosm
of the relationship and the communication within the relationship. To immediately abandon the closeness and physical communion during sex, in essence says, "Well, I've
gotten what I wanted; you as a person no longer interest
me."

Denise, a single woman, shared this story. Dissatis-
fied with her partner's lack of tenderness, although she
could accept his difficulties with erection, she decided to
stop being subtle and just ask her boyfriend Phil to hold
her after sex. He fidgeted for a few seconds, tried for a
moment, then jumped up saying, "I know, I know, I'm
just not compassionate. People keep telling me that but
that's the way I am. I always have been." She cried. He
left. When he finally called again weeks later, he told her
how angry he'd been with her. He blamed her for having

irrational needs and making demands. Then, Phil admitted that he realized his anger was his way of not accepting responsibility for his behavior or changing it. He agreed to work on "his" problem. "Time will tell," said Denise.

It is difficult for men to do something they've been trained not to do. Children seldom see adults touching one another lovingly. So, men need to learn to do what they have actually not seen, what they were not encouraged to do. They have learned to deny the need for loving touching and now must learn that not only women and children, but they, themselves, need it, too.

The best family atmosphere is one in which all members freely, openly, and appropriately engage in displays of affection. At the very least, parents need to display affection for their children, if not for each other. We simply don't do very well socially or sexually if we fail to get the proper kind of loving touching early in life.

Another boon would be for women to be more assertive in asking for their needs to be met. They need to stop thinking, "If he really loved me, he'd know what I want." Most women want touching, holding, and caressing to be a part of the daily pattern of their lives, not just part of lovemaking. The average man doesn't comprehend how important consistent physical contact can be to a woman or to a child. He got less as a child so he tends to give less. Few men understand that foreplay for the woman consists of closeness when they share meals, work, television, or whatever. It begins when they awaken in the morning and ends when they say goodnight. It happens when one rubs the other's tired shoulders. Often this is what women really mean when they say they wish they had more "romance" in their relationship.

Even if both partners are "touchers," they still will have differences to work out. One may want more touching when depressed, while the other wants to be touched when things are going well. One may prefer hugs and the other massages. One may enjoy holding hands and the other sleeping spoon-fashioned through the night. One may be virtually untouchable when absorbed in work. For instance, I find that the only type of touch I desire when I'm really concentrating or creating is an occasional shoulder massage when I've stayed hunched over the typewriter too long.

Sometimes one feels affectionate and the other doesn't. It takes a lot of communication to forestall feelings of rejection. It takes understanding to cope with times when one of the partners needs to be alone, to have their own space. It helps to verbalize your needs to your partner, yet explain that it has nothing to do with him or her. For emotionally healthy people, this verbal reassurance usually eases any feelings of rejection or abandonment. Explore your needs, compromise, communicate. This can work wonders in a relationship. Use the activities in chapter 12 to explore your touching needs and those of your partner's.

Some people prefer that loving touching be completely separate from the sexual act: some want it before, some want it after, and some want it at all those times. The only way to know is to explore, experiment, discuss and be committed to meeting each other's needs. Many people, both men and women, are so unaware of their feelings that they don't know if they want any loving touching at all. Be childlike in your approach to learning about touching.

It always helps to remember that touching desires vary as much as people do. Some want hugs and hugs and hugs. Some like to nestle at night; others may snuggle while watching TV. Still others may prefer backscratching, foot massages, face stroking and so on. A woman named Kay told me that for years she has wanted her husband to hold her on his lap and rock her. He thinks this is silly although he happens to adore having his head and scalp massaged.

It is unlikely that anyone is going to have all their touching needs met all the time. Therefore, it is of utmost importance to find the most important needs and to negotiate with someone who will be willing to meet them.

One thing is for certain: once people get over their fears and misconceptions about loving touching, once they start exploring, reaching out and receiving, they will feel better. You may not always feel like having sex, but would you ever turn down your favorite way of being touched?

Sex without intimacy, tenderness, communication, and loving touching reduces the other to nothing but an object to be used. No one, male or female, likes being used or considered an object.

Touching gently, tenderly, lovingly would build true closeness and trust—what we all need as a basis for a satisfying relationship. Touching is so essential to an intimate relationship that to omit this potent form of communication is self-destructive.

9 ○ The Healing Touch

*Touching communicates love, consciously or un-
consciously and can trigger metabolic and chemical changes in the body that help in healing.
Tactile stimulation and emotions may control
endorphins—natural body hormones that control
pain and our sense of well-being.*

 If your child comes to you feeling sick, you
may reach out instinctively and hug him. If
a close friend feels depressed you might put
your arm around him as he talks. If your
spouse has had a bad day, you might pat
his or her cheek sympathetically. When your baby is ill,
you might sit and rock him for hours. We use touch to
demonstrate our compassion and our understanding, but
we also instinctively use touch to communicate and transfer our healthy energies to loved ones in physical or emotional distress.

Anytime we reach out to touch someone who is in
need, that touch is healing them on whatever level is appropriate for that person. Not only can we help physically
but also emotionally. Sidney Jourard, a professor at the
University of Florida before his death and a close observer
of touch, has said that when one person reaches out to

touch another, he really says, "I want to share, I want to help." And when the other allows this touching, she replies, "I want to share, I want to be helped."

Throughout our history touch has been associated with the most powerful and mysterious accounts of healing. As far back as 15,000 years ago, touch was used for this purpose. Pictorial evidence in Pyrenees cave paintings show this as do early rock carvings and papyrus paintings in China, Egypt, and Thailand. The healing power of Jesus often came through touch. His laying on of hands is referred to 12 times in Matthew, Mark, and Acts. The laying on of hands became known as the "King's Touch" in France and England, and other kings and emperors, as well as religious figures, were said to be able to heal. However, healing outside the Church has always remained suspect. Even within the Church it may have lost its effectiveness because eventually the physical contact ceased and was replaced by symbolic gestures. As multitudes were administered to, this powerful healing instrument of touch was lost to the Church when they stopped the actual laying on of hands and anointing with oil.

In our time, the laying on of hands has long been practiced in fundamentalist Protestant churches, primarily rural, southern and black. It is also experiencing a resurgence in more traditional churches.

In mental and physical health fields today, many workers and therapists use touching as a form of communication and as therapy. *It works well when used with the same sensitivity and care as other therapeutic methods.* This caution is important simply because once you remove touch from the church, then the taboo of sex becomes a factor. Care must be taken that the encircling cape of the sexual taboo does not become the burial cloth of the healing touch.

There are many ways that tactile stimulation proves to be healing. We have discovered that "wrapping" or swaddling instead of using an incubator has helped many premature infants to survive and thrive, and we know that touch becomes a great help for these infants who suffer from an interrupted fetal development track. Dr. Als of the Harvard Medical School says:

> "We've just discovered that if we simply touch a struggling and unstabilized infant on his open, splayed palm, he is encouraged to bring his arms in, to relax his tense shoulders and neck and to help himself find a comfortable position that will alleviate a very dangerous strain on his heart and breathing."

We know that babies who do not get touched, cuddled, or held will just "waste away" with *marasmus*. Dr. Rene Spitz of the University School of Medicine in Denver, Colorado, prescribed touching in foundling homes for babies who were listless, withdrawn, and very slow in mental and physical development. In another instance, pediatrician Dr. John Holt mandated that all babies must be picked up and cuddled five times a day, resulting in a drop in mortality and an increase in the sick babies who became well.

We know that physical contact extends our own longevity and cuts down on the number of visits to a doctor. We have confirmed scientifically that touch is a biological necessity, and we are finding that the mere act of touching can promote physical and emotional well-being. Science now can document what primitive peoples knew long ago: that touching has beneficial effects on the body's internal workings. At the University of Maryland Medical School and the University of Pennsylvania School of Medicine, doctors have discovered that heart rates change when people are touched and that holding the hands of people who are in deep comas or even paralyzed produces significant cardiovascular reactions.

I had just completed one of my Master's theses on the effects of touch on learning, but one of my professors, Jerry, was rather skeptical—open to the notion, but skeptical. Months later he stopped by my house to tell me of his personal experience with the power of touch. His father had suffered a serious stroke and lay unconscious in intensive care, surrounded by monitoring and respiratory equipment. Jerry had no conscious memory of ever having touched or being touched by his father, but he remembered something he'd read in my paper. He reached out and placed his hand on his father's head. The equipment seemed to go wild. Panic struck. He immediately found a nurse who reassured him that what he had done was helpful and that such a reaction to touch was common. As his father recovered, Jerry made it a point to touch him on every visit. One day, his father hugged him, a profoundly moving experience for Jerry.

Another time in a hospital as my uncle lay in a coma, the family gathered and made the permitted periodic visits to the I.C.U. However, once in the room they stood well back from the patient. I asked a nurse to speak to them about touching. She told them that many people in the medical world believed that touching and talking helped in the recovery of a patient. A comatose person still needs the contact and caring communication from his family and responds on a very deep level. The family was then able to draw closer and feel they were doing something helpful by touching. If you didn't see the movie *Dad* with Jack Lemmon, then rent the video. Several hospital scenes between father and son illustrate so well what I've just discussed and what this book is advocating concerning touching.

Volunteers touch, stroke, and regularly hold sick babies at the Case Western Reserve University hospital. After a sustained period of touching, the babies gain weight and become alert and thriving.

It is now believed that a Down's Syndrome child will walk earlier if he experiences a lot of maternal (and familial) hugging, touching, and stroking. Also, doctors at Harvard Medical School use a "brush-touch" sensory stimulation technique to decrease spasms and produce more normal muscle action in some cerebral-palsied victims. The "brush-touch" is exactly what it says. The fingers brush lightly across the muscles of the afflicted child.

For women in labor, touch makes contractions more tolerable and reduces the need for painkillers and anesthesia. I know from personal experience how valuable it was to have my husband's hand to cling to and his arms around me at times during labor.

Numerous experiments with rats have shown that those handled by their keepers on a regular basis are smarter, bigger, and live longer than the untouched rats.

Experiments on rabbits also reveal the healing power of touch. Atherosclerosis is a condition whereby cholesterol deposits gradually clog veins and arteries and result in vascular diseases of various types, including heart attacks and strokes. Dr. Larry Dorsey in *Time, Space and Medicine*, reports on a study with test rabbits that confounded experimenters. A certain group of rabbits demonstrated atherosclerotic changes 60 percent less than that of the overall group. Then they discovered why this group of rabbits was affected less severely. Apparently, one of the investigators liked rabbits and during the course of the experiment regularly took them from their cages and petted, stroked, and talked to them. Could this be a co-incidence? After all, this vascular disease deals with molecular processes, not the spirit.

In any case, a systematic controlled study was conducted. The rabbit group that was petted and talked to once again had a 60-percent-lower incidence of atherosclerosis. But still not satisfied, the experimenters repeated the study for a third time. Again the same results: "touching, petting, handling and gentle talking was a primary determinant in the disease process from which most of us will die—atherosclerosis."

Perhaps this disease in rabbits isn't analogous to the human form of the disease. How can we say that similar psychological factors come into play with us humans? The current physical explanations seem inadequate. Well-known risk factors for heart disease include: high cholesterol, diabetes mellitus, high blood pressure and smoking. Yet in over *half* of the new cases of this disease, none of these risk factors is present. So if physical explanations do not suffice,then there must be psychological factors at work. So, back to the rabbits and the touching, petting, handling,and gentle talking. If we did these things for humans, much disease could be prevented.

Animals not only help us see how we could prevent disease by touching; they also help in a more direct way. An increasingly popular phenomenon is called *Pet Therapy*. Although we humans have had pets for thousands of years, only recently have social scientists looked into the nature of humans' relationships with "companion animals" such as cats and dogs. The research indicates that something mutually therapeutic exists in these relationships. Pets relax us, help us communicate, comfort us when we feel down, and build our self-esteem.

Pets also minimize stress. Although our blood pressure goes up when we talk to another person, with pets this is not the case. Most of us talk to pets differently than we do people, often touching them at the same time. We freely give and receive touching with pets. Many propose that the touching is the most important aspect. We can touch pets immediately and whenever we want to. This shows that access to affectionate touch unrelated to sex is very important.

Pet Therapy is being used and studied in nursing homes, mental institutions, and hospitals. Pet ownership contributes to the survival of heart attack patients and other seriously ill patients. Cuddling and touching animals has a soothing effect, thus reducing stress levels. Pet ownership not only seems to play a significant if small role in helping heart attack victims recuperate but helps families handle conflicts and helps disturbed teenagers straighten out. The Humane Society of Colorado's Pike's Peak Region has a "Petmobile" to visit nursing homes. The residents touch, hold, and talk to these visitors who don't mind whether their toucher is male, female, attractive, unattractive, young, or old.

Mildred, a resident of a home for the elderly, had to give up her dog. Her husband had died and she was left feeling unloved and alone. "If I could just have a kitten, I'd feel so much better," she said. A 1983 law mandates that elderly residents of over 900,000 federally funded housing units can't be barred from owning pets. Enforcement will hopefully follow.

Touching is effective whether being given or received. Dr. Neil Solomon, in a medical column in the Los Angeles

Times, reports that in this "era of wonder drugs, tender loving care is still an important adjunct to treatment." He goes on to say that various studies have demonstrated that touching between health-care personnel and patients can be as effective as medicine. He says that holding, patting, or placing an arm around a shoulder can accomplish much and help make a nursing home more than just a warehouse for the aged.

Irene Burnside, a nursing researcher, after studying successful efforts by nurses in using a caring touch with patients, initiated her own "touch therapy" experiment. She used touch as a means to modify behavior. In group sessions with elderly regressed patients she would greet and say goodbye to each patient with an Indian handshake—while using a typical handshake gesture she would also place her other hand on top of the two clasped hands. She also laid her hand on patients' shoulders when she spoke to them, touched them as she passed out cigars, and even danced with some patients. Her observations revealed increased touching among the patients, better response to music, increase in eye contact, and less hallucinating, in other words, more response to other people and to their environment.

Toni Preston in the *American Journal of Nursing* reports observations of organic brain syndrome patients, who, when touched by nurses, began to respond with hand gestures and affection. These patients, although unable to communicate verbally, responded to affectionate and sympathetic nonverbal cues of facial expressions and touching.

We now know that *feelings of love generate physical events*. Touching communicates love and can trigger metabolic and chemical changes in the body that help in healing. Tactile stimulation and emotions may control endorphins, natural body hormones that control pain and our sense of well-being.

Traumatic injury is an area where touch can provide immense value. The Shriners Burn Institute medical personnel say touching functions as a major antidepressant that could very well aid in the production of endorphins. Sometimes touch is the *only contact* with burn patients. All the medicines and antiseptics in the world won't help if a patient no longer has the will to live. Medical professionals state that touch is one of the most important aspects of rehabilitation, whether for an acute illness or a severely burned patient. A nursing supervisor says that sometimes she rubs the only unburned part of a patient's body in order to stimulate his will to live. At times it may only be the top of a head or bottom of a foot. Touching, maybe holding the patient's hand, helps put his mind at ease, helps him relax, and stimulates his spirit so that his body responds and his pain lessens.

Touch can also help alleviate pain. When we ourselves hurt, we frequently rub or touch the site of pain, whether it be our head, our jaw, or our stomach. Actually, this touch reduces the pain impulse to the brain by providing other sensations to block them. So "rub away," say people at pain clinics!

However, there are additional explanations as to why touch aids in reducing pain. It has been suggested that many ailments, specifically chronic headaches, could be the way a person subconsciously asks for love when unable to ask directly. Dr. David Bresler, Director of the UCLA Pain Control Unit, suggests hugging as a remedy for headaches. It works also on other types of pain. It reduces arthritis discomfort and helps promote circulation and emotional stability in diabetics. Any health problem responds well to touch and it can provide a positive emotional state to aid the body in its healing process. The motivation to reduce fear, frustration and a sense of helplessness can be instigated by the use of touch.

One specialized form of touching that is re-emerging as part of the holistic health movement (caring for the *whole* person—mind, body and spirit) is massage. It is increasingly recognized as a valuable health-care practice. Massage was used for a wide variety of emotional and physical problems in ancient societies in India, Greece, and Egypt. It has thankfully survived through some cultures and is now enjoying a resurgence in our country. This healing form of massage is not to be confused in any way with the sexual "massage parlor."

The simple act of accepting someone for who they are in their body and caring for them physically through touch and massage can do wonders for a person's self-acceptance. As human beings, we relate to the world around us through our body. So many of us have so little acceptance of our body. We think it doesn't feel right and especially that our bodies don't look right because of its imperfections. I've been a participant in what we called "our body group." I've given facial, foot, shoulder, hand, leg and back massages and received such massages, and one common thread is that I and the others involved began to feel more accepting of our bodies. Women especially learned that their bodies can be accepted for what they are and just as they are. In the beginning, many were ill at ease and embarrassed to "expose" their body or any part of it to the scrutiny of another. Apologies swarmed at the beginning of massage sessions but were soon lost in the pleasure and comfort found in being touched.

Benefits of massage abound. Massage relaxes the body, thus reducing stress not only at the time the massage is taking place but by way of teaching the body how relaxation feels. It is a method of retraining the body to respond, not with tension, but with relaxation. Massage also increases circulation, thus releasing toxins from the body. It increases sensation and energy and promotes a general sense of well-being if done properly. Most importantly, massage is a massive tactile stimulation experience and can alleviate skin hunger and cure touch deprivation.

Massage can be a nurturing, sensuous experience. During the process, many discover unconscious tensions, release suppressed emotions, have memory recalls, as well as new and pleasurable sensations. There are suggestions and instructions in the latter part of this book for doing massage and finding partners to join you in touching massages. I urge you to explore this medium of touching to become more aware and appreciative of your body and its touching needs. Whether you need nurturing touch, need to learn how to relax, need to accept sensuousness or need to listen to your "body language" rather than your head, massage can be of immense benefit.

Married couples have a built-in massage partner if both are willing. One couple I saw in counseling were Karen and Jack. Both had health problems. He'd had insomnia for 18 years and had tried all types of remedies to no avail. She had the skin problem called neurodermatitis. They agreed to try at least 15 minutes of touching before bedtime every night. We planned a specific ritual for their use in administering nonsexual touch. After only a few weeks, his sleep had improved dramatically, and her skin began clearing up. They also reported that they felt closer to each other, and their sex life was wonderful once again.

In addition to the use of massage, using counseling

therapy for skin problems can be of benefit. Besides the value of helpful support from a sympathetic counselor, any emotional difficulties aggravating or underlying the skin condition can be dealt with. As discussed in chapter 2, our skin produces symptoms as a cry for help, as a plea for attention to an inner distress.

What I call "internal touching" via the use of relaxation (with or without biofeedback), visualization, and hypnosis can be of enormous benefit. Sometimes, simply relieving daily stresses by regular relaxation exercises is enough. Sometimes more is required.

The following "internal touching" visualization exercise proved to be healing for many of my clients. It can be adapted for your specific skin problem. To assure success, it is necessary to engage the right hemisphere of the brain, sometimes referred to as the unconscious mind. This part of the brain directly accesses the autonomic nervous system that regulates breathing, heart rate, blood chemistry, digestion, tissue regeneration and repair, immune and inflammatory responses, and other bodily functions essential to our health and well-being. The language of the right hemisphere is imagery not the spoken or written word. Therefore, the exercise should involve the imagination and bypassing the left hemisphere could be achieved by having the process taped or spoken to you by someone else. An alternative is to purchase an already prepared healing tape, such as I have offered in the appendix.

1. Relax by using any type of breathing, meditation, or muscle relaxation procedure. A relaxing and easy to remember breathing technique is to:

(a) Make the *in*halation the longest breath by counting or by estimating;

(b) Make the *ex*halation the longest breath by counting or by estimating;

(c) Make both breaths the same length by counting or estimating;

(d) Eliminate the pause between the breaths;

(e) Observe how you breath naturally.

2. Visualize (imagine, fantasize, perceive or even think about — it isn't necessary to actually have inner "vision") yourself in a beautiful nature scene with the sun above you coming closer and closer until you can reach up and direct it like a spotlight to different parts of your body.

3. Beginning with your left leg, direct the sun as you would a spotlight from your toes to your hipbone then back down again. Do this several times, each time imagining and feeling the warm, soothing, healing, effects of the energy of the sun. Then move to the right leg, toes to hipbone. Continue directing the sun up the spinal column and spreading throughout the torso then cover the left arm from shoulder to fingertips, then the right arm. Next move the sun up and down several times on each area, imagining and feeling the effects of the sun energy on your skin.

4. If for any reason, the sun is not an appropriate image for you, then use another image. Suggestions for other images could be:

• Gentle, stroking hands belonging to God, or someone who loves you;

• A soothing, cooling ointment; or

- A colored light such as pink for love, blue for calmness, green for growth. Whatever color you wish to imagine as most healing for your condition is what you can use.

5. Focus on any sensations produced in the skin by your particular visualization You might feel coolness, warmth, tingling, smoothness, or simply relaxation.

6. Now, see the skin in the affected area looking and feeling clean, clear, beautiful, and completely healed. This step is important.

7. Feel activating energy as a current of electricity coming into your body beginning at your toes and spreading upward all the way to the top of your head.

8. Stretch, open your eyes, and allow yourself to feel completely refreshed and healed.

Do this visualization exercise three times daily until the symptoms abate, then once daily until some time after complete healing. Thereafter, use the relaxation portion daily and the visualization with it once every few weeks.

Medalie and Goldbourt studied 10,000 males to determine the impact of various risk factors on the frequency of angina. it was discovered, surprisingly so to the researchers, that men with severe anxiety who perceived their wives as loving and supportive had half the rate of angina (pain) as those who felt unloved and unsupported. Imagine what the addition of 15 minutes of touching could do.

Acupuncture and acupressure are both considered sophisticated touching techniques. Practitioners of these methods say that they work by stimulating the flow of energy through the meridians or energy centers of the body. I know from having experienced both acupuncture and acupressure and practicing acupressure on others that these methods do work. My husband, J.C., recently had an inflammation of the sciatic nerve, a painful affliction. After I had used both acupressure and massage from hip to foot, he told me I'd helped more than all the medical treatments had. I've taught many of my clients and friends some simple acupressure techniques, and most of those that use them agree they are like magic. Following are some guidelines for using acupressure for some common problems. There are no side effects from their use.

ACUPRESSURE

The process of using the fingers and hands to touch particular points. This process is based on acupuncture, a natural healing system using fine needles to stimulate particular points on the body. Developed by the ancient Chinese, it was successfully used in their culture for many centuries and has recently come into use in our country, not only through the use of needles, but also with laser beams. It can be used to prevent illnesses, to maintain health, and to aid in treating a diagnosed physical problem.

The process evolved from the theory that an energy system circulates through the body in channels called meridians. There are twelve meridians, eleven of which have the same name as the organ to which they are related. In addition, there is a central governing meridian.

The theory states that when an energy imbalance develops in the meridians—either too little or too much energy—illness can result. Acupressure assists the body in balancing the vital life force of energy.

Acupressure may be slower and require more repetitions than acupuncture, but it is safe, free, simple, easy-to-apply, and effective for use by the layman. It is intended as a supplemental or preventive measure and not as a substitute for conventional therapy.

It has been observed that when some points of the body are stimulated, a person's EEG brain wave will intensify, and the theta brain waves, indicating deep relaxation, become more numerous. This suggests that the conduction of impulses toward nerve centers have a constraining effect on the cerebral part of the brain. This seems to verify the recent discovery of endorphin release as a result of stimulating acupuncture meridian points.

HOW TO USE ACUPRESSURE

By making contact with any tender or painful point, you immediately begin helping that organ or tissue. Anytime you find a sore spot on your body and don't know its name or purpose, treat it anyway.

You can use the tip of either your index finger or your third finger, reinforce your index finger with the third finger, use two fingertips side by side, or even at some points, use the tip of your thumb. Keep your finger-nails short and smooth, as you'll need to press hard.

Once you contact a sore or tender energy center, which denotes an energy leak needing to be corrected, massage in a fast, small, circular motion or push down in pulsing movements. Then, apply as much pressure as you can tolerate, firmly but not painfully. Continue pressure for a slow count of 20 to 30. You cannot overtreat. The longer and the more often you treat, the better. In severe or chronic conditions, treat as often as possible at first, and then taper off. The time required is determined by your own needs. When the tenderness disappears, the energy imbalance has been relieved.

It is best not to eat just before doing acupressure or to apply this technique while pregnant.

The following charts show contact points in certain locations, search for sore or tender spots in that area and treat as directed.

A. HEADACHE, NECK TENSION.

The A points (where the black spots are located) for treating headache or neck tension are situated at the depression just below the occipital bone ridge at the base of the skull. Massage with thumbtips or other fingers.

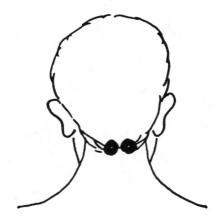

B. THE WHOLE BODY, TENSION, NECK/BRAIN CONGESTION, MENTAL FATIGUE, INSOMNIA, DIABETES, AND TO SOBER AN ALCOHOLIC.

The B points are located at the base of the neck on the trapezious muscle. Ask a friend to stand in back of you and place his thumbs, one on each side, on the points and press in and down toward the 7th cervical vertebrae (there is usually a slight protuberance at this vertebrae) at a 45-degree angle. This usually causes pain since almost everyone suffers from tension particularly in the shoulder area. You can do this for yourself by using the opposite hand to press down on the shoulder point. For example, using the right hand—with elbow held high-press the left shoulder with whatever finger is most comfortable to use.

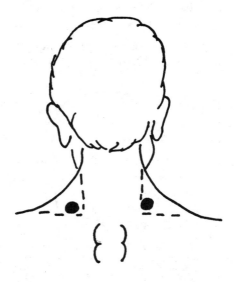

C. HEAD AND ARM PAIN, STIFF NECK. ALSO USE BEFORE TREATING THE MIDPOINTS (D) BELOW.

This point is located at the highest spot of muscle when the thumb and index finger are brought close together. Use your thumb to produce circular motions in the area shown in the diagram. Next press the point with the thumb aiming at the point but against the metacarpal bone of the index finger. Do both hands. A "funny bone" feeling (as when you hit your elbow on something) means you have found the right point. Doing these hand points first will enhance the effectiveness of any of the other acupressure points given.

D. ENERGY, BRAIN, SINUS CONGESTION, EYE-STRAIN, STOMACH, MENTAL FATIGUE, HEADACHE.

Treat the C points first. Now, locate the points that are shown closest to the nose bridge. These are located on the supraorbital bone as it joins the nose, usually at the beginning of the eyebrow. Using the tip of the thumb, slide the thumb straight back under the eyebrows, pressing upward.

Next, treat the midpoints (just beneath the middle of the eyebrow as shown), by applying pressure with the index finger. Treat any other painful areas in this general location. You can also use the knuckles on the midpoints until the pain abates. Congestion in these areas is one of the most common causes of headaches.

To me, the beauty of acupressure is that its use alleviates the sense of helplessness we sometimes get when we have pain or tension or it takes the place of reaching for a pill to take care of our symptoms. I use many such touching techniques, such as the acupressure ones I've just discussed, for myself. Sometimes the effects seem miraculous and, at other times, the effects are less. However, as I said, it costs nothing, is safe and easy, and requires very little time to use.

Another form of healing through touch is the laying on of hands, which some churches still practice. Other individuals using the power of touch to heal, call themselves "faith healers" or simply "healers." The common denominator among all healers is that the person doing the touching, the healing, believes he is a channel for some energy or power greater than himself. The energy could be labeled God, grace, life force, prana, chi, or by other names. The label doesn't matter as long as the healing works. Almost all healers feel they act as adjuncts to traditional medicine. Only Christian Scientists strongly discourage visits to medical professionals because they believe that illness is merely an illusion, since man is created in the image of God, and, therefore, perfect. For them, healing is a process of fully coming to this realization of unity with God.

There are a number of famous healers in this country, past and present. Katherine Kuhlman was one. She maintained that through her body, God dissoved tumors, let paraplegics walk again, and straightened twisted limbs. There are many who attest to her healing powers.

Another healer, Amy Wallace, who wrote the *Psychic Healing Book* with Bill Kenkin, believes, as do many that disease is a "dis-ease" between body, mind, and spirit. She calls upon the "oneness of things" in order to heal by physical touching or sometimes touch only with her mind and spirit.

Oscar Estebany was a world-renowned healer who never charged a penny for his work. While a Colonel in the Hungarian cavalry, he discovered that he could calm unusually skittish horses just by touching them. Later he worked for a veterinarian, alleviating discomfort in all kinds of animals. Then, he discovered that with people, he could put his hands on them and make the pain go away. Estebany believed that healing had to do with some kind of energy transfer. Laboratory experiments validated the healing ability of his hands when wounds on the backs of mice healed faster when he touched them. He also demonstrated that plants grew faster and more fully when exposed to his touch. When he retired, he offered his services for research purposes, and in Canada joined a group in which Dora Kunz, studying healing energies, was a member.

These two, Estebany and Kunz, and a medical doctor were joined in another study by the woman who is perhaps the best known "touch" healer in the United States today. Delores Krieger, a professor of nursing at New York University, is known for her study and development of "Therapeutic Touch." This method is derived from the laying on of hands to help or heal and involves using the hands to direct human energies. Dr. Krieger and a former student and colleague, Janet Macrae, have trained or overseen the training of thousands of health-care professionals in "Therapeutic Touch," as well as a number of lay people. Ten years ago, when I had training in "Therapeutic Touch," there were more than 5,000 practitioners in this country. Almost all of these people are nurses, although any highly motivated person can, to some extent, learn the practice. Dr. Krieger, as well as Dr. Macrae, believe that the ability to heal is a natural potential in everyone which can be actualized under the appropriate conditions.

The appropriate conditions include two variables crucial to the process:

1. The intent to help heal another, and

2. A fairly healthy body so that there is excess energy to channel.

Dr. Malcolm Todd, past president of the conservative American Medical Association, has said of "Therapeutic Touch," "Although the practice is difficult to assess, there is some element of success in what is being done. I am willing to have an open mind and see how it fits into traditional medicine."

Before I offer Krieger's explanation of how "Therapeutic Touch" works, let me point out that everything in the universe reduces to pure energy, which takes two forms, mind and matter. David Loye, in *The Sphinx and The Rainbow*, says, "Quantifying the ch'i of ancient Chinese thought and the prana of yoga, Einstein's most famous equation, $E = MC^2$, revealed the reduction of everything to energy, showing clearly that matter was compacted or congealed energy." Thus, our brains are the form energy took when compacted according to specific genetic codes.

Numerous articles have been written by and about Krieger. Her book, *Therapeutic Touch*, fully explains her method and theories. She maintains that our bodies constantly circulate and exchange energy and that this movement of molecules can be experienced by sensing the radiation of heat. In "Therapeutic Touch," this energy is transferred in a specific direction or modulation.

Hard scientific evidence backs up the effect of "Therapeutic Touch" on the patient's blood components. Specifically, controlled tests with touch were done on the hemoglobin (which helps deliver oxygen to body tissue, thus affecting health) values, and significant changes were found indicating the effectiveness of the treatment. Brain waves are affected, and a generalized relaxation response ensues during the touch treatment. Sr. M. Justa Smith, biochemist and enzymologist, hypothesized that if indeed an energy transfer did occur during healing, the change should be apparent at the enzymatic level, since enzymes are crucial to the basal metabolism of the body. The effects found were substantive, and all seemed to contribute to improving or maintaining health.

The practice of "Therapeutic Touch" is not claimed to cure but rather to boost or accelerate the healing process of the patient's own body. Some skeptics claim that although the touch feels nice, it elicits nothing more than the placebo effect which occurs when a sick person's condition improves through the use of a perceived treatment. However, even if that were true, the placebo effect itself is very powerful and shouldn't be denigrated. It has been shown to aid in over 30 percent of illnesses on which it has been tried.

For example, sick patients whose condition improves as a result of being given sugar pills rather than actual medication, are said to be responding to a placebo effect. Scientists and chemists aren't even sure how most of our present-day miracle drugs actually "cure." So if sugar pills help over 30 percent (with no side effects) that is certainly valuable.

"Therapeutic Touch" has been found useful and effective in treating circulatory diseases and upper respiratory problems, asthma, and other psychogenic diseases. Arthritis, edema, headaches, burns, gastrointestinal upsets, menstrual cramps, and tension have also been treated effectively. "Therapeutic Touch" is used for its relaxation effect before administering anesthesia, in cardiac units before insertion of cardiac pacemakers, on anxious dental patients, and to enhance wound healing. It is especially effective in relieving and frequently eradicating pain and in accelerating the healing process. Touch works well with all stress-related illnesses, which comprise 80 to 100 percent of all illness. It seems to have a significant effect on autonomic nervous system complaints: nausea, difficult breathing, rapid heart rate and poor blood circulation in the hands and feet. Clinical evidence shows that it increases the downward contraction of the intestines and helps relieve unexpelled gas and constipation. With babies, although the treatment must be shortened, "Therapeutic Touch" strongly supports the physiological development of premature babies and helps irritable infants sleep. The technique has been used with people experiencing an emotional crisis, helping to integrate their feelings and having a calming effect.

In order to be helped by touch, you do not have to be a believer. You can be as skeptical as you wish. The two factors that would prevent you from being helped by touch are denial of your illness or physical problem, and hostility. It appears that these two personality traits negatively affect the healer's efforts.

Briefly, the process of "Therapeutic Touch" according to Krieger consists of four steps:

1. Centering to prepare for the healing.

2. Assessing and scanning the body for differing sensations.

3. Unruffling any congested areas.

4. Consciously directing healing energy.

At the end of this chapter there is a somewhat more detailed and adapted version of "Therapeutic Touch" if you would like to try your hand at it. It is safe, free, and you can even use it on yourself in an emergency or when no one else is available to do it for you! However, it just feels nicer for someone else to do the touching.

Perhaps you've been in the mountains or near a waterfall and have experienced feelings of well-being. It is more than just the scenery producing the feeling. This well-being comes from something called negative ions. An ion is an electrically charged atom or group of atoms. When an ion contains an excess of one or more electrons, it becomes a negative ion, which can be beneficial to us. Machines which generate negative ions are highly touted and beginning to be more widely sold now. For over 60 years, We've known that ions affect the body but knowledge of the specific effects is still small. Positive ions, those deficient in electrons, seem to produce lethargy, headache, irritability, and inflammation of mucous tissues. The most extensive use of negative ion concentrations at the present is for burn therapy. As mentioned, the most naturally occurring areas of concentration for negative ions are near waterfalls and mountains.

Ions are related to "Therapeutic Touch" in this way. During the assessing phase, one sometimes encounters a feeling of static or dense energy, a congestion referred to as a "ruffled" field. As the hands move over the congested area, they pick up positive ions and remove them from the energy field.

This still leaves us wondering how the ions actually affect healing through touch. Now comes an exciting note. David Corey of Massachusetts General Hospital in Boston says, "The nervous system has lots of ion channels." Dr. Frederich Sachs of the State University of New York at Buffalo has found a new ion channel, which is the discovery of touch at the molecular level. When something presses into your skin, sensory nerves send a message to the brain. The nerves are fired, it is believed, by specific ion channels just newly discovered. This could be the fundamental mechanism for the perception of touch.

'These ion channels appear to be an essential mechanism by which the body communicates with itself, and individual cells communicate with themselves," says Dr. Sachs. This means that this cell-to-cell communication internally sets up the body as one large sensory organ.

This discovery could have implications for touch perception, hearing and balance, regulation of blood pressure, lung inflation, gut distension, cerebro-spinal pressure, organ stretch, and perhaps even homeostasis. Possibly, this could offer some explanation as to why touch is so crucial to one's health and well-being. These findings on ion channels were accidental, discovered during experiments with chick embryo tissue. We look to the future for more confirmation.

We can also ask ourselves if it is necessary to know absolutely and scientifically how something works, if it does produce results without side effects. In my use of touch for helping and healing, I've often been pleasantly surprised at the outcome. Touch has always been highly therapeutic and comforting, but people have become indifferent to its effects because in one way it is so common. I direct attention to the healing touch process by saying, "This might make you feel better," and it always does. I've felt better and so has the other person. The deep feeling of peace and relaxation after doing healing touch is enough to motivate me to continue.

When I work with a client in stress management, I always intend to help and to promote any necessary healing. Once, while a client was lying on my relaxation table and I sat by his side, I reached out and touched his foot, leaving my hand there for a few minutes while we discussed his problems. The next time I saw him, he asked if I'd touch his foot again. His neuropathy (a degenerative condition of the nerves due to diabetes) hadn't pained him all week. So the healing touch works even without conscious intent.

Of the people I have taught to use touch for healing, those who have practiced and persevered have benefited greatly, as do the recipients of their touch. At the end of the chapter is a list of benefits derived from using touch for healing. Read it carefully.

Throughout history touching has been connected with accounts of healing. Touching communicates love and as researchers point out, thoughts and emotions are biochemical events, so it is only logical that they would have biochemical consequences. Thus, the brain would be affected and influence other body organs through different thoughts and emotions.

Psychoneuroimmunology is a newly emerging field concerned with the relationship between psychological factors, the brain, and the immune system. We already know that a part of the brain, the cerebral cortex, influences white blood cells to do much of the immune system's work. Evidence is accumulating and hopefully will continue to show that metabolic and chemical changes in the body that help in healing, controlling pain and promoting a sense of well-being, come from our internal attitudes and mental states. So I say, the power of touch is that touching communicates loving, and loving is healing.

Find the form of healing touch you are most comfortable with. This might require investing some time and effort in reading, classes and practice. Then begin to use your abilities and skills to help yourself and others.

BENEFITS OF USING A HEALING TOUCH

1. No intervention into the body or surgery with the attendant risk and stress.

2. Economical in terms of time and money spent.

3. No side effects from medication, including aspirin.

4. Produces a state of communion with another human being. A release from loneliness. For the "healee," someone is doing something FOR you.

5. You are offering unconditional love and care to another.

6. Both the healer and healee will experience relaxation.

7. Pain and tension can be alleviated or eradicated.

8. Other ailments can be eased or helped to heal.

9. Circulation in the body can increase.

10. The healer gains a sense of value and effectiveness.

11. The healee is given a sense of self-responsibility.

12. Both the healer and healee feel calm and more centered.

13. Encouragement for the future is offered.

14. Both the health and health-care practices of the healed tend to improve.

USING A HEALING TOUCH

A common denominator among healers is that the individual feels he is the channel for a power greater than himself—an ENERGY. You might channel healing power from God, Christ Consciousness, universal energy, vital force, or as Delores Krieger believes, your own excess energy.

Do not be attached to the results. Remember, healers do not directly "cure." They channel energy to trigger the body's own healing response.

Practice every day on friends, relatives, and yourself for at least three weeks. After six months you will have a great facility for healing. Everyone has the capacity to heal, not all are motivated enough to learn to channel this ability, it requires much practice and awareness. Keep a journal of your experiences to validate the healing touch.

If you aren't feeling well, then it's not a good time to be a healer. You *can* heal yourself, but it's nicer and usually more effective to have someone else do it for you.

The person you are healing needs to cooperate by allowing you to touch them, but not to believe in what you are doing. In other words, if the person is skeptical but willing to "see what happens", proceed, if the person is resistant or hostile then make no further attempt to help.

FIVE CHARACTERISTICS OF AN EFFECTIVE HEALER

The first characteristic is a **sense of purpose**. You need to have a goal, so you know what you want and what you are going to do.

Second, **you need to possess self-discipline** in order to spend the time and effort required to read, learn and practice to perfect the skills involved in healing by touch.

Third, **you need to be compassionate or motivated** in the interests of the person you are healing. You need to come from a space within of unconditional love rather than your own ego needs. Since energy wrapped up in your emotions is directional, your motivation directs the energy.

An ability and willingness to confront yourself

with the truth of why you desire to heal is an important fourth characteristic. Healing is a powerful instrument, so know yourself and your power needs well. Why do you want to do it? Be truthful with yourself. The reason is important, but even more important is the asking of the question and being willing to see the real reason you want to use touch therapeutically.

Health, in the sense of wholeness and harmony within the self, is the fifth characteristic.

The quality of clairvoyance is not necessary to be an effective healer and so I won't number it, however, if you have the ability to "see" the subtle fields of energy and to reach with your mind directly and clearly for the information that is needed, your effectiveness can be greatly enhanced.

DOING THE ASSESSING PROCESS

If you already know where the problem or pain is, this step isn't absolutely necessary. It can allow you to become more sensitive in working with energy variations, perhaps detecting other problem areas that the person is unaware of. In the beginning it can be used to see if you can detect the problem area before you are told where it is.

Ask the person you are healing to sit in a chair with hands and feet uncrossed. Shake your hands to relax them, briskly rub them together, and then stretch the hands and fingers out fully for ten seconds. Then bring your hands slowly together and then back out. Continue this "bouncing" movement until you feel sensations in the palms. You might feel warmth, cold, tingling, pulsations, or feel as if you have a "ball" between your hands. Now place your hands on the person's head.

There should be no talking during this process. You are going to shift from left-brain hemispheric activity to right-brain, and talking interferes with the process of switching. Now you begin to disengage from outside thoughts and center yourself. If you are not familiar with ways to relax the body and engage the right-brain activity, then use this method. Put your chin on your chest, take a deep abdominal breath and bring your head up and back. Breathe out. Repeat this until you feel relaxed or centered. Ask the person sitting to do the same.

You will now begin scanning the body to look for and assess variations of temperature from one side of the body to the other. Move your hands with palms facing the seated person, at a level of two to three inches from the skin. Move your hands back and forth, starting at the head and moving slowly down. Do the front of the body, then the sides, and then the back (signal the person to stand for this). Move slowly but steadily. If you are unsure of an area, recheck that particular area after completing the feet. This should take about 45 seconds to a minute from head to toe.

Don't worry about warm or cold and what the temperature means; just look for variations. When you are finished, tell the person what you felt. In turn, the person may share what they were experiencing physically in those areas. It should be noted that even old injuries may produce temperature variations.

When the scanning is completed, sweep your hands from head to toe to relieve congested areas. This congestion may feel like pressure, dead space, static pressure,

denseness or heaviness. You will be especially able to detect a congested area where there is pain or tension, as in
the neck and shoulders. Afterward, shake or wipe your
hands to get rid of any positive ions picked up. Your
hands may feel dirty or "gunky." You may even wish to
wash your hands.

During the assessing and healing process, you will
usually feel more sensitivity or energy flow in one hand.
Use this as your healing hand, the energy conductor or
channel for the energy flow.

CHANNELING HEALING ENERGY

Ask the person you are healing to sit in a chair or to
lie down with hands and feet uncrossed. Make sure both
of you are in a position where you can comfortably sit or
stand for a prolonged period with your hands on the area
to be healed.

Ask the person to center himself and to visualize, as
you will be doing, the energy coming into their body. Or
give them a specific imagery of the healing process that
must occur in the body. Another alternative is visualizing
that the area is completely healed and functioning perfectly. The visualization by the person who is going to be
healed has two purposes:

1. You don't want to encourage others to be dependent
   on you. Ask them to not only use the visualization while
   you are working but afterwards as well.
2. Visualization is beneficial in and of itself as it has a
   definite effect on the body.

You are now ready to channel energy to areas of pain, disease or tension. Although Delores Krieger teaches placing the hands two or three inches from the body, I suggest directly touching the skin or clothed body unless you feel it inappropriate or difficult to reach the area involved. By directly touching, it brings the element of human contact and comfort. I prefer touching to almost touching.

Place one hand on top of the area, and the other on the bottom, or side-to-side, as on the neck. If you have not already discovered which is the healing hand or conductor, choose one for now. You will soon know which one it is. Perhaps, both are.

Center yourself by the breathing technique previously mentioned, or use your own technique. Now begin to visualize the source of energy you have decided to use as coming in through the crown of the head. This could be the sun, the light of God, Christ Consciousness, or another energy source. See this energy source coming through the crown of your head and down into the middle of your chest around the heart. Then direct it into the healing or conducting hand. See the energy moving into the area to be healed. Direct it into and through this area, and visualize the area healing.

Continue this channeling process for at least three minutes or until you feel other indications, such as the hands being pushed away or a temperature change. Do not worry about continuing too long. The body will only take in as much energy transfer as it needs.

If, once you start, you feel you're not in the right place or need to work on another area, move to where it "feels" right, where the energy is blocked, and continue. Use your intuition, your impulses, and feelings of the right-brain hemisphere.

The energy system will stay unblocked until the person blocks it again by environmental, chemical, or mental-emotional stressors. The person being healed may need to get other areas straightened out before they fully benefit from the healing touch.

During the beginning or learning period, practice every day on at least one person. If you absolutely can't find someone to do the touching with, practice on yourself. However, once friends or family members have experienced the relaxing and calming effects of this laying on of hands, you may have as many volunteers as you could possibly want.

Teach others to perform this process, so as many people can benefit from it as possible.

10 ○ Touching and the Workplace

Why should we limit ourselves by only being human in certain places or situations? Human beings go to work every day and human beings need touching.

Not surprisingly, touching can be quite a thorny issue in business offices and other places of work where power and friendship coexist uneasily. One man said rather sadly that he'd often like to put his arm around a young woman at work that he feels fatherly toward, but he doesn't dare. In another instance, a woman named Kay was upset because after working up the courage to tell her boss how angry she was at his unfairness, he patted her on the head, smiled and said, "Now, now." Needless to say, she didn't consider that a friendly touch.

We could speculate that because the business world is still primarily a male domain, it is also a touch-avoidant area. Because of the numerous problems with sexual harassment, touching in the office is too open to misinterpretation. The Gay Movement also adds to the problem of misinterpretation.

I read recently about a man I'll call Dave who was fired from his position as a staff psychotherapist at a hospital in the East. His crime was hugging. Dave saw hugging as a "nonverbal statement that we are all connected."

Lured to the staff job by a wonderful man, who was also later fired, Dave found himself in contact with a director who said that greeting new patients with a hug wasn't therapeutic and that hugging was an "overt acting out."

Dave had a history of hugging. When he was young, he and his brother raced each other every day to see who would get to hug Dad first. Dave spent his adolescence trying to mediate disputes and bring a little peace to his corner of the world. After Army service, he worked with street gangs in New York. Then, after more school, he took over a sort of in-state peace corps and taught at a university. His background and specific accomplishments are pretty impressive and didn't seem to be a factor in his being fired. It seems the hospital director just didn't like hugging.

Dave contends that we Americans are starved for loving because of our alienation from ourselves and the lack of contact with our empathetic, intuitive selves. I agree, Dave, and I say "Hurray, let's have more 'overt acting out.'" In this case, though, 57 year old Dave headed for California and new horizons where people have more accepting attitudes.

Lee, a coordinator of a health-care clinic, rhapsodized about a young nurse on her internship who gave the best back rubs. She made it a point to get one from this nurse every day. However, when it came time for the young nurse's final evaluation, Lee considered marking herdown for inappropriate touching behavior.

"Why?" I asked. "I thought you loved it and were really hating to see her leave."

"True," she replied, "but that's me. Others on the staff don't know quite what to do with her. Some of them get pretty uptight. They aren't used to being touched."

Here, I presented my point of view. I maintained that if the coordinator wanted to discourage this young woman from touching, then she should downgrade her. But it seemed to me that the attitudes of some of the staff created the real problem. Obviously, they needed some touching education and experience. Even more, it would have benefited the whole group to get together and discuss the problem. I checked with the coordinator later, a warm, huggable person herself, and she hadn't said a word to the young nurse about "inappropriate touching."

Obviously, the act of touching is like any other message we communicate. It may elicit negative reactions as well as positive ones depending on the makeup of the people and the circumstances. Should we then be careful? Very careful? This seems to harken back to the days when we heard "don't touch," "watch out," and "be careful." We are no longer children. When will the warm, loving people carry more weight than the cold and distant ones?

It seems to me that if we are respectful and aware and use common sense, then we shouldn't have much trouble touching whomever and wherever we want. That is, after we get over our terribly inhibited touch-avoidant upbringing!

Among the places of work I spent considerable time in were public schools. The following is the preface to a thesis I did with the academic title of *A Survey of Nonverbal Communication Research In The Areas Of Warmth And Touching Behaviors As Related To Teaching*. I call this particular part "The Warmth of Touching in School."

Sometime during my early years of teaching, I became conscious of the fact that students were really responding to my nonverbal communication. Without a word, they seemed to sense that I liked them. I became aware that people, particularly students, responded to touch and often a smile, a physical closeness. A touch seemed to break through the barriers that others set up to defend themselves and made it easier to communicate.

Many incidents come to mind regarding the effects of nonverbal communication and especially the power of the human touch. There were times when the initial attempt at touching was rejected but later the student would put himself or herself in a position to be touched and would often reciprocate.

Once a gentle embrace of another's shoulders allowed a girl to release pent-up emotions that had caused her to stop coming to school. Another time, a student teacher came to me for help. He couldn't get our speech class to settle down and pay attention. It took so much time and hassle, he sometimes felt like giving up.

I went to the classroom with him and for the first ten minutes we circulated among the students, sometimes just smiling at them, at times stopping to check on assignment progress or answering questions, but ALWAYS TOUCHING the student in some way. We might touch on the head, the shoulders or arm or hand before moving on. When we finished and moved to the front of the room, every student was sitting quietly and looking very attentively toward us. I smiled at him, touched him on the arm and left. The student teacher was amazed at the results. He repeated this pattern of action on other occasions and in other classes. The result was always the same.

Similar reactions occur when students are working at their desks, and I occasionally would circle the room and touch each student (unless they signaled they didn't want to be touched). The students then were quieter, appeared to concentrate more and get more work done.

If a teacher is concerned with humanizing education, with facilitating the communication and learning process, then the teacher will need to become aware of her own body language and become adept at understanding the body language of others. Unfortunately, our culture often teaches children to distrust their own instincts and senses. Thus, the teacher may have to work at undoing a great deal of negative training in themselves and in their students.

Nonverbal acts called warmth cues and touching can be used as honest expressions of emotion. If they are not honest, many students would soon detect the difference. This would occur because the body, operating on an unconscious level of awareness, would soon give itself away by sending the real message which would be contradictory.

A word of caution in connection with touching. It is a powerful force and because of this a teacher will no doubt encounter some students, parents, administrators and others in a community who are frightened or who misinterpret the use of touch. To use touching in the classroom would require knowledge, much courage and tact. Intent is very important, also.

I have been lucky, possibly due to my age and sex. The maternal image is more acceptable in our society when touching is involved. The male in any grade level and the young female in secondary schools would conceivably face more problems. Our society, as a whole, still equates touching with mothering and sexuality. Perhaps, as teachers become more knowledgeable of all areas of nonverbal communication, we can make giant strides in changing ideas and mores by giving information and by demonstrating touch as something caring, comforting, and healing.

At a recent speech convention, I attended a session on nonverbal communication. The lecturer covered many diverse areas and talked of the activities he used to teach, but when I asked him about touching, the man threw up his arms, shielded his body momentarily, took two steps backward and said in what seemed to be a tighter voice, "Oh no, I would never have anything to do with that." At first I thought he must be kidding but he was serious. This attitude, unfortunately, reflects that of many people, including teachers.

I found through my research and confirmed through my experiences that touching facilitates communication and learning. However, in teaching, as in other workplaces, we encounter the cultural taboos and restrictions on who touches whom and where.

Recently, a journal reporting on a new type of Cranial-Sacral therapy developed by a doctor of osteopathy, noted that the staff psychiatrists at a famous mental healthcare institution, after a demonstration of the therapy, were very concerned. Not about the efficacy of the procedure but about whether they could do good psychiatry if it involved touching their patients. This attitude is not limited to psychiatrists but is also prevalent with psychologists and counselors in many settings.

There is cause for optimism. In California's Silicon Valley, known as a caldron of stress, a new employee benefit for stress reduction has been instituted. At Apple Computer and other companies, a health-service company offers either as a company perk or at minimal expense, a mini-massage as an alternative to caffeine and sugar breaks. During break time the employee sits on a stool and has his entire back, including shoulders, arms, back, neck, and scalp massaged while fully clothed. It relaxes and energizes the employee. Apple says this stress reduction method fits in with their overall program to promote fitness. It also meets a need for touch whether the employee recognizes that need or not.

More and more companies are allowing similar services, such as the mini-massage, to be offered. According to a friend who does on-site clothed mini-massages and other reports, one serious drawback seems to be the soundproofing of the room that is used for the worker's stress reduction session. Customers and other workers complain the oohs and aahs of delight are distracting.

Ken Blanchard and Spencer Johnson based their popular book, *The One Minute Manager*, on the best of research in the fields of management training, interpersonal relations, motivation, and discipline. Well-known in management training are the theories of X and Y styles of management. The X manager's interest lies in results, while the Y manager's concern is with people. Both have disadvantages. Japan developed a managerial style known as theory Z, somewhat of a compromise between X and Y styles, based on a delineation of a set of characteristics that the most effective long-term manager should possess.

Blanchard and Johnson's allegory of the One-Minute Manager is a viable alternative to X and Y theories of management and an answer to Japan's Z theory. This new management theory incorporates something new and valuable to management, that helps people, work morale and productivity. This new and valuable addition is touch. Two techniques, one-minute praising and the one-minute reprimand, are both designed to train people to be winners. Both techniques conclude with touching. Managers are told that at the conclusion of the "motivating" session the employee should be touched briefly in a friendly way to let him know you are on the same side as he is, and as a way of giving something—reassurance, support, or encouragement.

Management consultant Elaine Yarbrough and University of Colorado professor Stanley Jones say that contrary to the popular belief that physical contact at work is a no-no, using touch can increase your effectiveness. After analyzing more than 3,000 individual touches, they concluded that neutral touching on the shoulder or arm is most acceptable as are brief touches of no longer than ten seconds. Touching another person makes it more difficult for them to turn down a request and affirms the bond between two people. Understanding touch effectiveness is of particular importance to women since touch initiation is associated with power. Therefore, a woman's touch is seen as evidence she has power, too.

The Farmers' Almanac, known for its long range weather predictions and common-sense advice, started a pro-hug campaign. The 73 year old editor, Ray Geiger, passed out "free hug" coupons while touring the country. These coupons are good for one hug and redeemable from any participating human being. I've gotten several from different people who said they were circulating in their workplace and wondered where they originated. The almanac urges hugging as a way to relieve stress. Bumper stickersreading "hugs not drugs" are also part of the campaign.

Ray's quota of twelve hugs a day is subject to certain rules. The hug should be compassionate, not passionate, and you should always ask first. Hugs, he says, are a way to come out of America's ice age. I like this kind of businessman.

As a counselor in private practice, I have found touching to be an invaluable way to ease sorrows, allay fears, establish contact, as well as trust with clients. However, there are some clients that for various reasons I rarely or never touch. Nor do I believe that all therapists should touch. Touching should be done only if the therapist is open, willing, and quite comfortable with touching and convinced that it will benefit that particular client at that particular time and place. In other words, touch is not to be used as a technique or as an intellectual approach.

Ethical Issues reports on several studies by Holroyd and Brodsky concerning therapist and client interaction. The therapists who engaged in nonerotic physical contact the most were humanistic therapists and the least touching were the psychodynamic, behavior-modification or rational-cognitive therapists. Approximately half of the therapists agreed that nonerotic physical contact would be appropriate and beneficial in four categories of clients:

1. Socially or emotionally immature, such as a history of maternal deprivation;

2. Those in acute distress, such as grief, depression, or trauma;

3. For general emotional support and;

4. For greeting or at termination.

In one study of 657 therapists, the researchers concluded that when the older and more experienced therapists are doing the touching, it does not lead to intercourse with the client, and that the most common practice related to intercourse with clients is the restriction primarily by male therapists of touching to opposite-sex clients. However, only about 27% of the respondents in one study occasionally engaged in affectionate touching because of various taboos. This is despite the acknowledged therapeutic value in many cases.

We've been discussing touching in the workplace. Why should we limit ourselves by only being human in certain places and certain situations? Human beings go to work every day, and human beings need touching.

11 ○ The Helping Touch

My mother rubbed my neck. I knew she must love me.

 The helping touch is all too often a rarity rather than a common occurrence. From questionnaires and from interviews, I gathered some brief descriptions after asking the question: *Can you think of a special time that touch has helped you in some way?* The answers are in each individual's own words and are identified by sex and age only.

FEMALE, 16: *When I was in the hospital after a bike accident, I needed to be touched—my friends did some. It helped me feel loved.*

FEMALE, 54: *When I touched my mother as she lay ill. I was able to hold her and tell her I loved her. I had never told her that before. It made her "beam." I'm glad I did it, It comforts me now knowing I did. She died.*

MALE, 32: *A series of visits to a chiropractor after a car wreck. It helped my back to heal.*

FEMALE, 25: *When I was real depressed and down after a fight with my husband, my kids sat in my lap and hugged me and made me feel needed and loved.*

MALE, 33: *When I am upset it would help if someone held my hand.* **No one ever has.**

FEMALE, 18: *When I was 15, I got pregnant and it was the end of the world for me. I wasn't dating like all my friends, I felt fat and ugly and I got NO affection from anyone. Then Mike felt my need; he just held me. He's the only guy who took me anywhere. Now we plan to be married.*

MALE, 37: *I discussed my anger and frustration at work to get some sort of relief, and I got a pat on the back. It made me feel better.*

FEMALE, 62: *When I was depressed and my children helped by putting their arms around me.*

MALE, 50: *A male co-worker massages me on the neck and shoulders and back when I'm really tense.*

FEMALE, 30: *Once when I was angry and upset, someone touched me, and it made me stop and think.*

FEMALE, 17: *I was really upset—my mother and I had been fighting. My best friend then (David) just cradled me in his arms and held me tight. It was wonderful!*

FEMALE, 22: *My best friend and I got into a fight and for a long time I was really upset. We usually don't fight and this was a big one. I worried. We looked at each other for a while and then we just hugged. That hug said so much!*

MALE, 49: *Touch helped before and after heart surgery. It helped me feel someone cared.*

FEMALE, 57: *When my son died, it helped and then when my mother died. They were feeling touches. They felt close and warm and I knew they were sincere.*

FEMALE, 16: *When I was about to cry, my boyfriend touched me around my chin and cheeks and hugged me.*

MALE, 30: *When I come home after a week of traveling, my wife sometimes has me lay in her lap and she strokes my face and hair. It really feels good.*

FEMALE, 19: *I had some medical problems and I was really scared and Scott rocked me and I felt so much better.*

MALE, 48: *I was on the Board of Directors of a 1,500-person singles group twelve years ago and I proposed that everyone on the Board wear a badge to identify themselves and have unlimited permission to kiss anyone at a function. There was no dissent. I was the primary practitioner of this "rule." This is my rhyme: Kisses are free. They're free from pollution. The more you give away. The more you have to give.*

FEMALE, 34: *I was suicidal and my lover held me for two hours while I cried. He said he liked my tears, loved me and the closeness helped him, too.*

MALE, 45: *The phone rang late at night and I was told my father had had a severe heart attack and wasn't expected to live. My wife didn't even ask for details; she just put her arms around me and started kissing and touching. We ended up having sex, and it was the best I ever had. She made me feel I'd be okay.*

FEMALE, 28: *I was feeling totally worthless and my therapist touched me on the shoulder and then kissed me on the cheek.*

MALE, 20: *I'd gotten in a lot of trouble, even spent the night in jail and when I got home my mother rubbed my back. I knew she must love me.*

12 ○ It's Okay to Touch—
Activities and Ideas

In the first two minutes you renew contact with someone you care about, touch him in a caring way.

 So how do you know if it is okay to touch someone? I talk about this issue in workshops. Some people are so uptight, suspicious, frightened and deprived that sometimes, if you really want to touch or hug someone, you have to just take your courage in your hands and do it! Anytime is appropriate as long as you don't harm or interfere with the other in a negative way.

It may help to tell the person that you know he or she doesn't really feel comfortable with touching but you really need it. This is the way I started with my sons. With my older son, Jaye, remember, at first he wouldn't let me within a foot of him. Things progressed so far that after he moved out, he'd come over almost every day for a hug. However, if you feel you need guidelines, try these:

1. Be aware of the person and the situation.

2. Look at the person's face and body, discern what their body language tells you. If they look tight, cold or fearful then tread lightly.

3. As you approach the person or begin to reach out, look at the person's face. If he averts his eyes or draws his chin down, that could well indicate he isn't going to feel comfortable being touched.

4. You might want to announce your intention or make a request.

5. If you decide to go ahead and touch, touch neutrally at first. Neutral points include the elbow and top of the shoulder.

6. Assess the reaction to this neutral touch by looking at the person's face and body.

7. Do whatever you feel fairly comfortable with at this point.

A SPECIAL NOTE: Never continue touching someone time after time if they don't like it or if they don't eventually reciprocate. It is okay to get someone used to touching, to help them release inhibitions, but at some point you need to receive also. Once a person is used to touching and enjoys it, then you have a partner with whom to share some of the activities in this section.

How many hugs a day do we need? Sidney Simon, author of *Caring, Feeling, Touching,* says three, others say four or five. The late Virginia Satir, well-known family therapist, believed eight or twelve are needed. I believe we need as many as we can possibly get. At the end of a workshop one afternoon, I asked everyone to hug as many people as possible in the next ten minutes and then added,

"And of course, I'm open to hugs, too." I gathered up my materials, turned to speak to someone at my side, hugged two people behind me and then looked around. There must have been 40 people already lined up! I hugged over a hundred people that day. It felt wonderful! When I taught, after a few weeks in a class I became accustomed to getting an average of 25 hugs a day. I never got too many. I never reached the surfeit point. Only you can know what your body and heart and mind need, and you will only know by experimenting and doing. Happy discovery to you!

On the following pages you will find ideas and activities for touching with people you care about, with people you know well like spouses, lovers, friends, parents or children and with people you don't know well. Try out all of them.

TOUCHING ACTIVITIES

SHARE YOUR TOUCHING HISTORY FROM CHILDHOOD TO THE PRESENT. Do this with a new friend or an old friend. The following suggestions are only to help you begin. The important part is sharing and becoming consciously aware of where you've been in regard to touch. Include messages you've heard or your experiences in regard to the following:

- Touch
- No-no's
- Types of holding you've experienced
- Bathing (remember childhood sponge baths?)
- Clothing and its feel

- "Feel pieces" or security objects
- Dating
- Parents touching you
- Parents touching each other
- Touch and pets
- Touch with same-sex friends
- Why it is easy or not easy to touch
- Why it is easy or not easy to be touched
- Favorite ways to be touched
- Touching with significant others in your life now
- Feelings about touching

When you do this activity, try sitting back to back with your listener and closing your eyes. Don't discuss. You talk and when you finish, let your partner share his history. *Then* you can discuss.

DECIDE IF YOU ARE MORE LIKE A CAT OR A DOG IN REGARD TO TOUCHING. Dogs are usually eager to be petted and readily available. They also reciprocate in their own way. Cats want what they want when they want it. Think of some more differences. Observe pets, or ask questions of friends who have pets.

HAVE PARENTS, FRIENDS, OLDER CHILDREN, OR YOUR SPOUSE FILL OUT A COPY OF THE QUESTIONNAIRE IN THE FRONT AND BACK OF THIS BOOK. Compare their answers with yours and discuss them.

SHARE YOUR PRESENT NEEDS AND FEELINGS ABOUT TOUCH. Do this with someone non-judgmental who will not be threatened by your needs. Later, when you are more sure of yourself, share these feelings with all those close to you.

SURPRISE SOMEONE WITH A FOOT MASSAGE and then ask him to reciprocate. If you're as fastidious as I am, you'll want to wash your feet just before and have the other person do the same. An alternative is to do it for each other with a small pan of water and a washcloth or with apple vinegar and cotton, making a little ritual out of it. Don't forget the ankle and heel areas in the massage. If you are interested in health as well as pleasure, invest in a book on foot reflexology which will show what areas of each foot correspond to what areas and organs of the body and how to treat sore or tender areas. Better yet, invest in a professional reflexology treatment (they are inexpensive usually) and then you'll know how to do it for someone and can teach them to do it for you.

DISCUSS A TIME WHEN TOUCH HAS BEEN MAGIC (out of the ordinary) for you. Do this with a partner. Then trade off.

TRY A "DIFFERENT-TYPES-OF-TOUCH" WEEK. Pick out a week or even just a day to experiment with all the different kinds of touches you can think of. Even try some sneaky ones with grocery clerks, waiters, babysitters, and so forth. Keep a record to share with someone later. Don't tell anyone what you've doing until you finish with the experiment.

DO A FANTASY DAYDREAM accompanied by beautiful, slow and peaceful music. Imagine a beautiful temple. Leave all your inhibitions and clothing in the vestibule. Enter different rooms, each being a different color. You can experience any kind of touch from anyone you wish in each of the rooms. Enjoy!

ASK FOR A TENSION RELEASER. The first time you feel shoulder and/or neck tension, ask the first friendly person you are with to see if they can find the special points on the shoulder used to release tension. (There really are some—see the diagram below.) Then change positions and reverse the process. A little extra massaging won't hurt. While standing over the person, use the thumbs to press firmly down and inward. Tell the person to breathe deeply since it will hurt more if they are tense. These are tender points. Hold the pressure for about 30 seconds then massage and do it again.

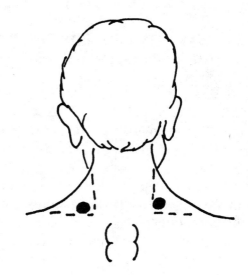

GIVE SOMEONE A FACIAL MASSAGE and then let him give you one. This can be absolutely delightful and relaxing. Afterwards, your skin will glow and you'll look younger. You will find instructions in the appendix, or you can order a tape I've recorded with full instructions called *Facial Massage for Partners* (see the tape list in Appendix B). Anytime you are doing any type of massage, be sure to find a quiet, comfortable, warm place and play soft, relaxing music. A candle or incense or both add to the soothing atmosphere.

TELL YOUR FAMILY YOU ARE DOING A SURVEY ON SKIN STIMULATION and need to know what feels best to them: scratching, light tickling, light or firm stroking, circular rubbing and so on. Use their back to demonstrate and check out each type of touch. Then ask them to try this on you. If you really want to appear serious about this, be sure to approach each member holding a notepad and pen and list of different types of skin stimulation!

TREAT YOURSELF TO A FINGERTIP FACIAL MASSAGE. You can use the instructions in the appendix and if desired, there is a tape available to guide you called *A Self Finger-tip Facial Massage* (see tape list in Appendix B).

DO A RAIN DANCE ON SOMEONE'S HEAD with your fingertips. Simulate a few sprinkles, a light shower, then bigger rain drops, and eventually a thunderstorm. Be adventuresome, sing "Raindrops Keep Falling On My Head" while you are doing it! Yes, this is sort of corny but it usually makes people laugh which releases that nervous tension about being touched in a new way. An alternative would be playing a recording of rain and thunderstorms.

Of course, when you are finished, ask the person to reciprocate!

ASK FOR A HUG IN A GROUP. Do this exercise in some safe, *familiar* group of which you are a part. Don't explain, just pick someone out and walk up and say, "I really need a hug. Would you give me one?" You will rarely be refused if you read nonverbal signals before asking. Try touching the person you are asking lightly on the arm as you ask. You can explain afterward if you want. If you are inhibited about touch and fear rejection, you will really benefit from this. Get a friend to do the same as you and then you can discuss it afterward. Have fun with it!

EXCHANGE BACK MASSAGES with someone. Use oil to make your fingers glide. Get a book on massage and follow the directions, or do what would feel good to you. Don't forget the neck and shoulders, especially the tops of the shoulders.

GIVE SOMEONE A TEMPLE MASSAGE. Stand close behind your partner and tip his head back against you at a comfortable angle. Gently brush and caress and stroke the temple area from beneath the eyebrows into the hairline. Imagine you are removing all the stress accumulation of the day or all the worries lodged in the area. When you finish, *gently* squeeze his head and return it to the original position. Then take your hands away so slowly he can't quite be sure when they actually leave. Wonderful for headaches and tension.

DO A TENDERNESS TOUCH on someone by cupping the other's face gently between both of your hands and looking softly into his eyes and smiling. Think tenderness while doing this.

HAVE A PROFESSIONAL MASSAGE. If you've never been to a masseuse or masseur, go to one or have one come to your home. Health clubs and hotels often offer massage. Pretend you are a baby, take off all your clothes—you'll be covered with a sheet—and enjoy! If you think you can't afford it, ask for it as a birthday, Christmas, Easter, Fourth of July, or whatever, gift. Consider it a gift of health and well-being.

DO A TRUST CIRCLE. Gather at least eight people together. Have one person stand in the middle of the circle—start with someone small—hands at side, and fall backward. The people on that side of the circle all join forces and catch the "truster" by using their hands and arms to support head, back, and legs. This requires a cooperative group. Then the person is "rolled" around the circle, first facing out, then with the person facing in to middle of the circle. Lots of touching here. It is advisable not to make joking comments during this exercise. Do not do the exercise unless the atmosphere is one of caring. Take special care not to drop or hurt the "truster".

DO A BLANKET ROCK for a child, someone frightened or distressed or just someone you like. The lucky one lies down on a blanket while the others (how many others depends on the weight of the person being rocked) stand around the edges of the blanket and pick up the edges firmly and securely. You may want to kneel or squat as the blanket and person within doesn't need to be lifted but a few inches from the floor. Begin to gently, as a group, rock back and forth and to and fro. It may help to desig-

nate a "rocking" leader to coordinate efforts. Sing a lul-
laby to make this extra special. Everyone ought to hug the
rocked person afterward. The results from this exercise
are extraordinarily nurturing. When you ask "who's next"
there is usually plenty of volunteers.

EXPERIMENT WITH HUGS. Try different types and
lengths of hugs. Notice which you like best and when, if
ever, you want to stop hugging. Kathleen Keating has a
darling book with bear illustrations called *The Hug Therapy Book* that illustrates different types of hugs. For now
try:

1. A side-to-side hug with arms around each other's
   waists;

2. An upper chest hug with your behind stuck out;

3. A distance hug with at least six inches between your
   bodies, and;

4. A full heart-to-heart and full body contact hug.

When I do a workshop on touching, I usually scan the
audience before I begin and pick someone to come up and
demonstrate hugs with me. This person will exhibit nonverbal cues that indicate they would be open to touching
and, very importantly, look gentle. One day I became so
involved in talking to people as they came in I forgot to
pick my demonstation hugger. When it came time, I
looked around but from the back of the room came a loud
voice, "I want to do this demonstration, I'm a great hugger." A man who looked as big as a bear walked down the
aisle, leaned down, put his arms around me, lifted me

against his chest, and at least a foot off the floor and squeezed hard. I heard and felt a rib pop. As soon as I could breathe, I asked to be released. That man thought he was a wonderful hugger! I admit, the motivation, energy, and feeling was there but his technique certainly needed improvement. So read and practice proper hugging ways.

WRITE YOURSELF A HUG PRESCRIPTION. Be daring and sign it as if you were a doctor (illegibly). Make the prescription for as many hugs as you want but at least five hugs a day. Explain to people that it is a serious health matter and don't crack a smile when you show them the prescription.

USE THE HEALING TOUCH on someone who needs it. The instructions are in chapter 9.

WRITE SOMEONE A HUG. Pick out someone you care about and write him a note that says, "I'm sending you a big hug." Be really adventuresome and appear at someone's doorstep with those words on a sign!

EXCHANGE HAND MASSAGES WITH A FRIEND OR YOUR SEXUAL PARTNER. Have your partner sit comfortably, eyes closed. Take their hand in yours and begin to *gently* push, press, and massage, at times pressing in the palms so the hand automatically stretches out. Work the areas between bones and tendons well. At the end lightly stroke both tops and bottoms of hand with your fingers drawing out the stroke past the tips of your partner's fingers. As the diagram below shows, start at the X and follow the arrows for front and back of the hands.

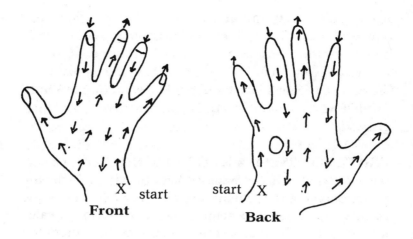

Front   **Back**

Press often on the spot shown by a circle (the fingers will automatically curl inward when you press there). This is a wondrously enjoyable massage. Trade back and forth after each hand is done so you end up with both of you having both hands massaged.

EXPERIMENT WITH LIGHT AND DARK. Try cuddling or hugging someone, first in the light and then in the dark. Discuss the different emotions and physical sensations that you find. Even try going into a closet and staying with someone there for at least 10 or 15 minutes.

TELL YOUR PARTNER WHAT YOU WANT. Again, with your sexual partner, do a hand massage. But this time you have to tell him exactly what you like and want, the pressure, type of stroke, where to touch and when, what you'd like him to try, how it feels. Use phrases like "I'd enjoy . . ." or "I'd like you to try . . ." or "I find this pleasing, would you continue touching just like that."

Then trade until both of you have had both hands massaged. You can find out a great deal about each other in this nonthreatening way.

USE A DIFFERENT KIND OF TOUCH THAN IS CUSTOMARY FOR YOU. If you usually shake hands, try using both hands in an Indian clasp by using one to cover the handshake. If you don't usually shake hands, do it. Try touching people on the arm as a greeting or the neck or the face or the shoulder. This is appropriate in any work situation. If you don't hug, try that. We tend to get in ruts; climb out for a while.

BE AN OBSERVER FOR A WEEK and keep on the lookout for people touching. Sit in a coffee shop, in a park, or in a car on a busy pedestrian street. Take notes, and if you come up with something unusually interesting, let me know. My address is at the back of the book.

CUDDLE YOUR PET. Give your dog or cat a little extra touching, if it will let you. You'll both benefit. If you don't have a pet, try this on someone else's pet but be warned, you may make a friend for life.

HAVE AN "EMOTIONAL TOUCH" DAY. Pick out a particular day, and for every emotion you experience, touch yourself or someone else to express how you are feeling. The only cautions are for anger and sexual desire. Be discreet. Remember, don't tell anyone what you are doing. Well, okay, maybe one friend who won't tell anyone else. No words, just touch. For example, having a bad day? Then lay your head on someone's shoulder and sigh. She will get the message. Check out what you learned about yourself by doing this exercise.

EARLY CONTACT. In the first two minutes you make new contact with someone you care about, touch him in a loving way. This could be morning, evening, or whenever you come together. Try this for a week without telling him what you are doing and see what happens.

MAKE AN "I NEED A HUG NOW" BUTTON or name tag and wear it all day. Also, smile a lot.

HELP YOURSELF GO TO SLEEP by asking someone to give you a back rub before bedtime. If you don't have someone who lives with you, invite a friend to stay the night or have a "bunking party." Many insomnia problems have been cured this way.

FIND SOMEONE TO SHARE TOUCHING WITH. If you need someone to do some of these exercises with, pick out a likely candidate, loan him this book, and then ask if he will share some experiences with you. Each of you pick the activities you want most.

GATHER A GROUP. Form a group that meets once a week or month to do touching activities. I belonged to one and everyone really enjoyed the experience. We took turns being the facilitator and choosing what we would spend time doing. Sometimes we taped exercises so we could all participate at once. An important part should be discussing at the end of each session how you felt about the activities. The next two activities could be done in a group that has met for some time and who are comfortable with touching:

PRETEND YOU ARE A BABY. Have someone rock you and then you can rock him. The rocker person needs to sit with back supported and legs apart. The "baby" puts his bottom between the outstretched legs and lies against the chest with his face in the curve of the partner's neck. A little soothing, nurturing, affirmative talk really adds to this but isn't necessary. If you like, play the *Nurturing Yourself* tape found on the tape list. Have a good time with this and use your imagination.

TRY A ROCKING THREESOME. Use the procedure in the "Pretend you are a baby" exercise, except that the third person will gently stroke the face, neck and arms of the one being rocked. All three get a turn at being rocked.

TRY NONSEXUAL TOUCHING WITH YOUR SEXUAL PARTNER. Ask your sexual partner to let you touch her or him for one hour in any way you want (no genital touching) without any conversation and without it ending in sexual activity. Turn the lights down low, put on some soft, relaxing music, light a candle and incense, and just enjoy touching and pleasuring your partner. Afterwards, ask your partner to pick the time he or she wants to do this for you.

TRY A VARIATION ON NONSEXUAL TOUCHING. Do the previous exercise, but ask your partner to tell you how she or he wants to be touched.

FIND A HOT TUB OR SPA. Perhaps a friend has one, or fill your tub with hot water and bubble bath and enjoy the sensuousness of the feeling against your skin. Light a candle and turn the lights out. Music provides a wonderful background for your water-touching time.

WATCH A MALE CONTACT SPORT. It doesn't matter if it's on TV or in person. Remember, these are primarily men who aren't "touchers."

DO A MIRROR DANCE WITH A PARTNER. Stand or sit facing the other person, standing is preferable. With fingertips touching, both close their eyes and one leads. Then reverse. Express caution, hesitancy, freedom, anger, love, nurturing, and caring with your fingertips. Now try it again. But this time try following the leading person's hands without quite touching. Keep your eyes closed. Discuss what it felt like to do this.

FOR SMOKERS ONLY. If you are a smoker, before each cigarette—okay, every other one—run your fingers slowly across your lip, top and bottom, 10 or 20 times. That's it. I'm not asking you to quit, just to try this. With your lips and fingers touching you are activating two of the largest tactile areas of the brain. These are the same tactile areas involved with lighting and smoking a cigarette. I noticed when I quit smoking how much I missed that stimulation. Perhaps, it can provide you in a nonharmful way some tactile stimulation you are needing.

LOVE YOUR BODY. Stand in front of the mirror in the nude, and stroke your body from head to toe. Don't criticize your body while you are doing this. Accept it and love it.

STRESS REDUCTION TOUCHING. Demonstrate to someone how touch can reduce stress. Pat, stroke, and rub one of his bare arms from hand to shoulder for at least two minutes. Then ask him to compare the touched arm with the untouched arm. The touched arm usually feels lighter, more tingly, relaxed, or better in some way. This is how a well-touched, unstressed whole body could feel. While you are touching, tell him about touch and what you've learned from this book or how you feel about touching. When finished, switch so you can experience this feeling as well.

BE CHARITABLE. Visit a home, institution, or hospital with elderly patients or children and offer to give some of these people a back rub, foot or hand massage, or whatever you are able to do the first time. Please don't neglect the less attractive people or the older men. These people usually get left out.

BABY MASSAGE. If you don't have a baby, find someone who does and offer to give the baby a bath. Also give it a baby massage while you also wash, dry and powder.

BEGIN AN EVENING FAMILY RITUAL OF TOUCHING. It doesn't have to last long. Each person gets to decide what he wants done each evening, or each person gets a special night to decide what everyone does. Approach this as solemnly as possible. Make it a real *ritual*. Set aside a special time and place. Have oil available. Use a timer; otherwise those who really get into enjoying the touching will swear they are being shortchanged. Ignore any protests when you begin this activity.

PRETEND YOU ARE A MASSAGE THERAPIST AND GIVE A FULL BODY MASSAGE to someone as a special gift. Read a book on massage first if you aren't sure what you are doing. Act like a professional, and be sure the setting, lighting, surface, covering, privacy, music, etc., is just right. Be sure to keep the fortunate person well covered except for the area you are working on.

READ ABOUT TOUCHING. Be sure everyone you care about reads this book or some book about the need for touching.

GOLDEN LIGHT HUG. If you are already a hugger, try this: using full body contact and a heart-to-heart hug, think about all the good qualities of the person you are hugging. Then imagine the two of you surrounded, filled, bathed, by a beautiful shimmering, golden white light from above. Hold the hug extra long. If you are not already a hugger, try this anyway. Share your feelings with others after you've finished.

OPENING YOUR HEART. Sit facing a loved one with your eyes closed. Hold both his hands. Imagine your heart with a double door in the middle of it. Ask your partner to do the same. Now, both of you imagine opening this door as widely as you can and silently invite the other to enter and explore what he finds in there. After some time has lapsed, gently and lovingly imagine reaching out your index finger and touching the heart of the other. (**CAUTION:** This may sound like a very simple exercise but it can be very intense and extremely moving emotional experience. Ask yourself if you are truly ready before you try this process.)

WRITE TO ME if you have questions, comments or stories to share. My address is in appendix B. Thank you for letting me share with you.

Appendix A ○ How Do You Feel About "Touch" Now?

Please answer the following questions based on how you think and feel after having read this book. It is my sincere hope that you have had an opportunity to let the ideas and information sink in and to do many of the activities and experiments suggested.

1. What *now* comes to mind with the word "touching?"

2. How would *you* define touching?

3. Whom do you touch regularly now (outside of sexual activity)?

4. On what part of the body do you now touch people? List the people and the body parts.

5. Where would you like to be touched (list person and body part)?

6. How and when do you now want to be touched?

7. Are you aware of feeling skin hunger? When and how often?

8. What do you do when you experience skin hunger?

9. Tell about some awareness you now have, based on your observations of others' need for touch.

10. What restrictions do you still feel about touching others? For example: time, place, person, daylight/dark.

11. What restrictions do you intend to work on eliminating?

12. Do you remember any particular time or times when touch has helped you or has been "magic?" Tell about it briefly.

13. What could you do to encourage people to touch more? What people in your life need to touch more?

14. Are you touching and being touched as much as you want?

15. How many hugs a day do you want? How many are you getting now?

16. Would you prefer the act of sex or just holding, stroking, and cuddling? Why?

17. If you could tell your partner honestly, no holds barred, two things about touching and lovemaking that you want him or her to know for your benefit, what would they be?

Appendix B ○ Cassette Tapes by Phyllis Davis

Facial Massage With Partner

Narrated instructions on giving a step-by-step facial massage with time to relax and enjoy before trading places. You are guided through a special beginning and ending to the massage to make it especially pleasurable.

Self Fingertip Facial Massage

This tape guides you through a soothing, nurturing, relaxing facial massage that you can give yourself.

Nurturing Yourself

Within each of us is a small child needing reassurance, approval, love, and encouragement. This is an "inside touching" tape. After relaxing to prepare the mind and heart to listen, you hear nurturing messages that we all need to hear to achieve better self-esteem. Side two is the nurturing message without relaxation so you can listen often while working, driving or reading.

Long Progressive Relaxation

Learn to relax and refresh yourself by following these instructions to tense and relax specific muscle groups in the body. Develop awareness of when tension is present and how to release it. After the step-by-step instructions an opportunity to visualize a calm, peaceful scene of natural beauty is followed by soothing water sounds. This visualization time can also be used for touch fantasies or meditation. Use this tape for a "pick-me-up," times when you're feeling stressed, or as a terrific way to lull yourself to sleep.

Healing Visualization

Visual imagery can change our physiological state! The body can actually respond to a mental picture as if it were a real experience. After relaxing the mind and body, you are guided to direct healing light into your body and to specific problem areas and then to picture the area as perfectly healthy.

ORDER CASSETTE TAPES FROM:

Transformations
Phyllis Davis
1701 Misty Lane
Lee's Summit, MO 64063

Send $12.95 plus $1.30 postage and handling for each tape. Satisfaction guaranteed or return within ten days for refund of purchase price.

Bibliography

BOOKS

Ayres, A.J. *Sensory Integration and Learning Disorders*. Los Angeles: Western Psychological Services, 1972.

Barkey, L.L. and N.B. Collings. Nonverbal and Kinesic Research in *Methods of Research in Communication*. Emmert & Brooks (eds.). Boston: Houghton Mifflin, 1970.

Blum, Ralph. *The Book of Runes*. New York: St. Martin's Press, 1982.

Burgoon & Saine. *The Unspoken Dialogue*. Boston: Houghton Mifflin, 1978.

Bresler, David and Richard Trubo. *Free Yourself From Pain*. New York: Simon and Schuster, 1979,

Carter, Mildred. *Body Reflexology*. West Nyack, N.Y.: Parker, 1983.

Corey, Gerald and Mariane S. Corey. *Issues and Ethics in the Helping Profession*. Pacific Grove, CA.: Brooks-Cole, 1983.

Dossey, Larry. *Time, Space & Medicine*. Boulder & London: Shambhala, 1982.

Downing, George. *The Massage Book*. New York, Random, 1972.

Durden-Smith, Jo and Diane Desimone. *Sex and The Brain*. New York: Arbor House, 1983.

Farrell, Warren. *The Liberated Man*. New York: Bantam Books, 1981.

Grossbart, Ted and Carl Sherman. *Skin Deep: A Mind/Body Program for Healthy Skin*. New York: Wm. Morris, 1985.

Gunther, Bernard. *Sense Relaxation*. New York: Pocket Books, 1973

Harlow, H.E. *Learning to Love*. San Francisco: Albion, 1971.

Henley, Nancy. *Body Politics: Power, Sex and Nonverbal Communication*. Englewood Cliffs, N.J.: Prentice-Hall, 1977.

Jourard, Sidney. *Disclosing Man to Himself*. Princeton, N.J.: D. Van Nostrand Company, 1968.

Keating, Kathleen. *The Hug Therapy Book*. Minneapolis: CompCare, 1983.

Klaus, Marshall and John Kennell. *Maternal Infant Bonding*. St. Louis: C.V. Mosby Co., 1976.

Knapp, Mark. *Nonverbal Communication in Human Interaction*. New York: Holt, Rinehart and Winston, 1972.

Koneya, Mele., and Alton Barbour. *Louder Than Words: Nonverbal Communication*. Columbus, Ohio: Charles Merrill, 1976.

Krieger, Delores. *The Therapeutic Touch (How to Use Your Hands to Help or Heal)*. Englewood Cliffs, N.J.: Prentice-Hall, 1979.

Lair, Jess. *Sex: If I Didn't Laugh I'd Cry*. New York: Fawcett Crest, 1979.

Leboyer, Frederick. *Birth Without Violence*. New York: Alfred A. Knopf, 1982.

Loye, David. *The Sphinx and The Rainbow*. Boulder: Shambhala, 1983.

Lynch, James. *The Broken Heart: The Medical Consequences of Loneliness*. New York: 1977.

Masters, William and Virginia Johnson. *The Pleasure Bond*. New York: Bantam Books, 1976.

Mayo, Claro and Nancy Henley.,(eds). *Gender and Nonverbal Behavior*. New York: Springer-Verlag, 1981.

Macrae, Janet. *Therapeutic Touch: A Practical Guide*. New York: Alfred Knopf, 1988.

Medalie, J.H. and V. Goldbourt. Angina Pectoris Among 10,000 Men II: Psychosocial and Other Risk Factors as Evidenced by a Multivariate Analysis of Five-year Incidence Study. *American Journal of Medicine*. 60, 1976. 910-921.

Meerloo, Joost. Rhythm in Babies and Adults. Basmajian, Haig A. (ed.) *Rhetoric of Nonverbal Communication*. Glenview, Ill.: Scott, Foresman and Company. 1971, 58-60.

Montagu, Ashley. *Touching: The Human Significance of the Skin*. New York: Harper & Row, 1971.

Morris, Desmond. *Intimate Behavior*. New York: Random House, 1972.

Naisbitt, John. *Megatrends*. New York: Warner Books, 1982.

Restak, Richard. *The Brain: The Last Frontier*. New York: Warner Books, 1979.

Rinlen, Robert and Karen Gravell. *Deciphering the Senses: The Expanding World of Human Perception*. New York: Simon & Schuster, 1984.

Schneider, Vimala. *Infant Massage (A Handbook For Loving Parents*. New York: Bantam Books, 1982

Simon, Sidney. *Caring, Feeling, Touching*. Hadley, MA, Values Associates Press, 1990.

Thompson, J. *Beyond Words*. New York: Citation Press. 1973. Watson, John B. *Psychological Care of Infant and Child*. New York, 1928.

Young, Michael. The Human Touch: Who Needs It.

J.Stewart (Ed.). *Bridges Not Walls*. Reading, Mass.: Addison-Wesley, 1973.

Zunin, L. and Zunin, N. *Contact: The First Four Minutes*. New York: Ballantine Books, 1976

JOURNALS, MAGAZINES, AND PAPERS

Aguilera, D.C. Relationships Between Physical Contact and Verbal Interaction Between Nurses and Patients. *Journal of Psychiatric Nursing*, January-February, 1967, 13-17.

Bauer, Bernard. Skip the Coffee Break, Have a Massage. *Kansas City Star*. April 30, 1985.

Boderman, Alvin, Douglas Freed and Mark Kinnircan. Touch Me, Like Me: Testing an Encounter Group Assumption. *Journal of Applied Behavioral Science*. 8-5, 1972.

Breen, James. Bonding Isn't a Prerequisite for Devotion. *Kansas City Times*. March 25, 1984.

Brody, Jane. Bonding at Birth: Theory Gets Second Look. *Kansas City Times*. March 31, 1983.

Burnside, Irene. Touching is Talking. *American Journal of Nursing*. 72–12, December, 1973.

Casler, L. The Effects of Extra Tactile Stimulation on a Group of Institutionalized Infants. *Genetic Psychology Monographs*. 71, 1965, 137-175.

Chance, Paul. A Touching Story. *Psychology Today*. May, 1987.

Clay, V.S. The Effect of Culture on Mother-Child Tactile Communication. Columbia University. PhD. dissertation, 1966.

Davis, Phyllis K. A Survey of Nonverbal Communication

Research in the Areas of Warmth and Touching Behaviors as Related to Teaching. Central Missouri State University. Master's Thesis, February, 1978.

Edwards, D. The Value of Touch in Psychotherapy. *American Journal of Orthopsychiatry*. 52, 65–72.

Farrell, Warren. Risking Sexual Rejection: Women's Last Frontier? *MS*. April, 1982.

Firing Doesn't Stop Therapist From Hugging. *Kansas City Star*. August 3, 1983.

Fisher, Jeffrey, Marvin Rything and Richard Heslin. Hands Touching Hands: Affective and Evaluative Effects of An Interpersonal Touch. *Sociometry*. 39–4, 1976, 416–421.

Frank, L.K. Tactile Communication. *Genetic Psychology Monographs*. 56, 1957, 123–155.

Grossbart, Ted. Bringing Peace to Embattled Skin. *Psychology Today*. February, 1982, 55–60.

Harlow, H.E. and R. Zimmerman. Affectional Responses in the Infant Monkey. *Science*. 130, 1959, 421.

Henley, Nancy. Power, Sex and Non-verbal Communication. *Berkeley Journal of Sociology*. 18, 1974–74, 1–26

Hewitt, J. Liking for Touchers as a Function of Type of Touch. *Psychological Reports*. 50, 1982, 917–918.

Hibbard, J.A. Attitudes Toward Sexual and Nonsexual Touch in Dating Couples as a Function of Level of Romantic Love. Purdue University. Master's Thesis, 1974.

Hockaday, Laura R. Pet Project: Therapy Program Takes Army of Animals to Nursing Homes, Hospitals for Visits. *Kansas City Star*. June 9, 1986.

Hollender, Marc. and A.J. Mercer. Wish to be Held and Wish to Hold in Men and Women. *Archives of General Psychiatry*, 33, 1976, 49–51.

How Men Feel About Sex: A Guide for Women. *Sex Over Forty*. II,6, November, 1983.

Jay, S. The Effects of Gentle Human Touch on Mechanically Ventilated Very-Short-Gestation Infants. *Maternal Child Nursing Journal*. 11, 1982, 199–256.

Jourard, S.M. and J.E. Rubin. Self-Disclosure and Touching: A Study of Two Modes of Interpersonal Encounter and Their Inter-Relation. *Journal of Humanistic Psychology*. 8, 1968, 39–48.

Kaiser, Robert. What Happened to a Teacher Who Touched Kids, *Look*. August 10, 1971.

Kershner, Bruce. Tracking the Sense of Touch. *Buffalo Physician*. July, 1985.

Klimek, David E. Kissing in Public: It's Abhorred or Adored. *Kansas City Star*. December 18, 1984.

Krieger, Delores. Therapeutic Touch: The Imprimature of Nursing. *American Journal of Nursing*. 75-5, May, 1975.

Krieger, Delores. Therapeutic Touch: Searching for Evidence of Physiological Change. *American Journal of Nursing*. April, 1979.

Landers, Ann/Creators Syndicate. Most Women in Poll Say They are Happy Just to Be Held. *Kansas City Times*. January 15, 1985.

Liebowitz, Kenneth and Peter Anderson. The Development and Nature of the Construct Touch Avoidance. Paper presented to *Speech Communication Association Convention*, 1976.

Macrae, Janet. Therapeutic Touch in Practice. *American Journal of Nursing*, April, 1979.

Miller, J.A. and J. Silberner. Ion Channels: Touch at the Molecular Level. *Science News*. 127, 406.

Naisbett, John. *Megatrends*. 1982.

Nguyen, Michele, Richard Heslin and Tuan Nguyen. The Meaning of Touch: Sex and Marital Status Differences. *Representative Research in Social Psychology*, 7, 13–18.

Nguyen, Tuan, Richard Heslin and Michele Nguyen. The Meanings of Touch: Sex Differences. *Journal of Communication*. Summer, 1975, 92–203.

Pattison, Joyce. Effects of Touch on Self-Exploration and the Therapeutic Relationship. *Journal of Consulting and Clinical Psychology*, 40-2, 1973, 170–175.

Pechter, Kerry. Pet Therapy for Heart and Soul. *Prevention*. August, 1985, 80–86.

Prescott, James W. Body Pleasure and the Origins of Violence. *The Futurist*. April, 1975.

Prescott, James W. Alienation of Affection. *Psychology Today*. December, 1979.

Preston, Toni. When Words Fail. *American Journal of Nursing*. 73-12, December, 1973.

Publication Embraces the Habit of Hugging. *Kansas City Star*. September 7, 1984.

Reuben, Carolyn. Craniosacral Therapy. *East/West Journal*. October, 1987.

Rosenfeld, Lawrence. Body Regions Generally Regarded as Accesible to Touch by Others. *Journal of Communication*. Summer, 1976.

Rosenthal, Vin. Holding: A Way Through the Looking Glass. *Voices*. Spring, 1975, 2–7.

Sachs, Frederich and F. Guharary. Mechano-Transducer Ion Channels In Chick Skeletal Muscle: Effects of Extracellular ph. SUNY School of Medicine. Buffalo, N.Y.

Sandhoff, Ronni. A Skeptic's Guide to Therapeutic Touch. *RN*. January, 1980.

Scarf, Maggie. The Promiscuous Woman. *Psychology Today*. July, 1980. 78–87.

Schaffer, H. and E. Emerson. Patterns of Response to Physical Contact in Early Human Development. *Journal of Child Psychology and Psychiatry*. 5, 1964, 1–13.

Silverman, A.F., M.E. Pressman and H.W. Bartel. Self-Esteem and Tactile Communication. *Journal of Humanistic Psychology*. 13, 1973, 73–77.

Solomon, Neil. Hospital Treatment Aided by Touching: A Doctor's View. *Kansas City Star*. April 3, 1979.

Spitz, Renee. Hospitalism: Genesis of Psychiatric Conditions in Early Childhood. *Psychoanalytic Study of the Child*. 1, 1945, 53–74.

Study Shows Forced Sex Accepted. *Kansas City Star*. September 22, 1985.

Thayer, Stephen. Hidden Messages of Touch. from Psychology Today in *Kansas City Times*. April 21, 1988.

Touching. *Current Health*. March, 1980. 20–22.

Walker, D.N. Openness to Touching: A Study of Strangers in Nonverbal Interaction. University of Connecticut. Ph.D dissertation. 1971.

Watson, W.H. The Meanings of Touch: Geriatric Nursing. *Journal of Communication*. 25, 1975, 104–112.

If you would like to receive a catalog of Hay House products, or information about future workshops, lectures, and events sponsored by the Louise L. Hay Educational Institute, please detach and mail this questionnaire.

We hope you receive value from *The Power of Touch*. Please help us evaluate our distribution program by filling out this brief questionnaire. Upon receipt of this postcard, your catalog will be sent promptly.

NAME _____

ADDRESS _____

_____

I purchased this book from:

☐ Store _____

City _____

☐ Other (Catalog, Lecture, Workshop)

Specify _____

Occupation _____ Age _____

We hope you receive value from *The Power of Touch*. Please help us evaluate our distribution program by filling out this brief questionnaire. Upon receipt of this postcard, your catalog will be sent promptly.

NAME _____

ADDRESS _____

_____

I purchased this book from:

☐ Store _____

City _____

☐ Other (Catalog, Lecture, Workshop)

Specify _____

Occupation _____ Age _____

To: HAY HOUSE, INC.
P.O. Box 6204
Carson, CA 90749-6204

To: HAY HOUSE, INC.
P.O. Box 6204
Carson, CA 90749-6204